Conventions in Contemporary Art

Lectures and Debates Witte de With 2001

Conventions in Contemporary Art

Lectures and Debates Witte de With 2001

Edited by Valentijn Byvanck

Witte de With, center for contemporary art, Rotterdam

Contents

Janneke Wesseling
Charlotte Huygens
Kitty Zijlmans

Els van der Plas

Valentijn Byvanck

Preface

The Netherlands has a modest intellectual tradition in the visual arts. The ideal of free expression has driven theory and practice apart, so that thought in art often seems opaque and unnecessarily abstract. In 2000 and 2001, Witte de With organized a series of debates that were meant to act as a counterbalance.[1] The debates focussed on general topics and provided a forum for artists, critics and curators. Oriented towards routines, assumptions and vogues in reflections on today's art, rather than vanguard positions and formal theoretical issues, they particularly targeted a set of ideas that circulate in the art scene and exert a powerful influence on established exhibition practices but are seldom or never subjected to critical scrutiny or exposure. The debates addressed such topics as the policies involved in the production of art in public places, the role of the curator in today's art, the encounter of art and design, and the place of non-western art in the western art world. For each debate, speakers were not only selected for their specific expertise, but also for their unconventional perspective on the topic at hand. The evenings kept to a fixed routine: two or three speakers gave a brief presentation, followed by a discussion with the audience.

This book provides an impression of the debates, but not a verbatim report. Some of the presentations, including Carel Blotkamp's contribution to *The Netherlands Imagined* and Thomas Levin's *Heterochronicity*, were published elsewhere.[2] Other presentations have been omitted because, however attractive and inspiring they were on the evening itself, they were too impromptu for the print medium or not suitable for this forum. The selection has made the book less complete but more rounded than the sum of the evenings. The directness of the spoken debate defers to the refinement of the written argument.[3]

1. All the debates published in this book took place in Witte de With and were chaired by Valentijn Byvanck. The forewords to the following debates are revised versions of the preparatory statements sent to the speakers.
2. Carel Blotkamp, "Identity/Reality," *The People's Art / A Arte do Povo* (Rotterdam: Witte de With, 2001), 24-36; Thomas Levin, "'You Never Know the Whole Story': Ute Friederike Jürß and the Aesthetics of the Heterochronic Image," in: Ute Friederike Jürß, *You Never Know the Whole Story* (Stuttgart: Cantz Verlag, 2000), 54-87.
3. All the speakers reworked their presentations into essays, with the exception of Catherine David, whose text is an edited transcription.

Many people contributed to the success of the Witte de With evenings. Jeroen Boomgaard of Amsterdam University, Roemer van Toorn of the Berlage Institute, and Witte de With's Solange de Boer, Tanja Elstgeest and Nathalie Zonnenberg acted as program advisors. Witte de With's previous director Bartomeu Marí provided the opportunity to set up the theory program. Gé Beckman, Paul van Gennip and Line Kramer provided logistic support. Ingrid Commandeur, Liesbeth Levy, Hein Reedijk and Iebel Vlieg advised me on the first debate on non-western art, Lex ter Braak on the curatorial debate. I further wish to thank Herman Verhagen for his prompt transcriptions, Ruth Koenig for her accurate translations, and Gracia Lebbink and Willem Morelis for their careful design and typesetting. Solange de Boer deserves special mention for her untiring work, sound advise and great eye for detail in all phases of this project. I am, however, most indebted to the speakers for putting up with lengthy preliminary discussions and correspondence and for not losing their temper or concentration with the sometimes sharp tone of the debates: Iwona Blazwick, Carel Blotkamp, Jeroen Boomgaard, Koen Brams, Catherine David, Anthony Dunne, Katalin Herzog, Charlotte Huygens, Sebastian Lopez, Thomas Levin, Bart Lootsma, Bartomeu Marí, Adi Martis, Alan Murray, Els van der Plas, Fiona Raby, Ineke Schwartz, Siebe Thissen, Janneke Wesseling, Camiel van Winkel and Kitty Zijlmans.

Debate I

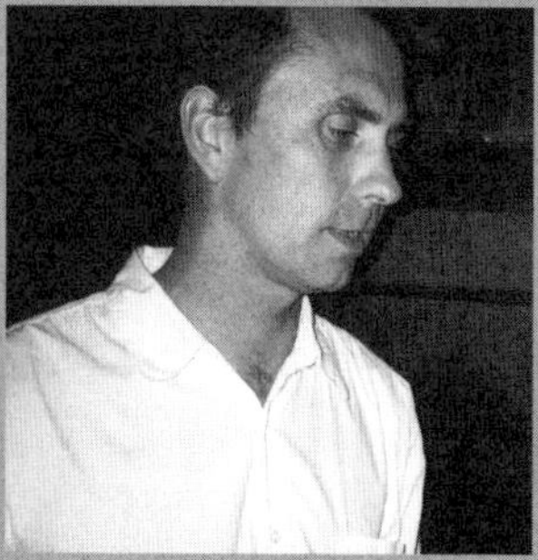

Camiel van Winkel

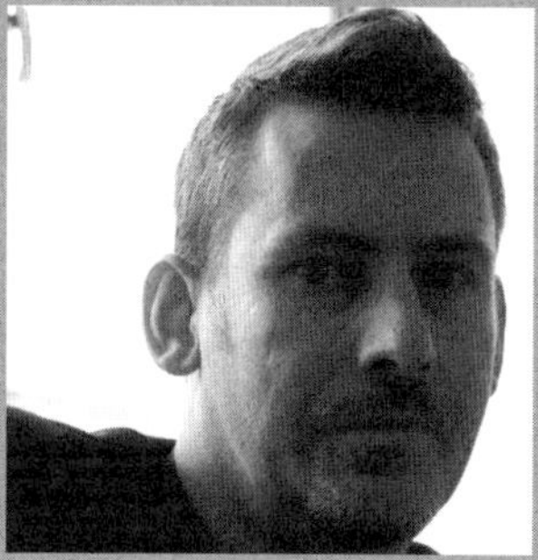

Bart Lootsma

Debate II

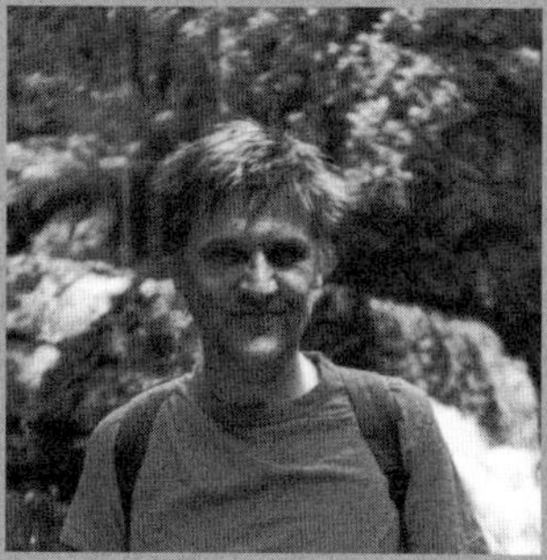

Jeroen Boomgaard

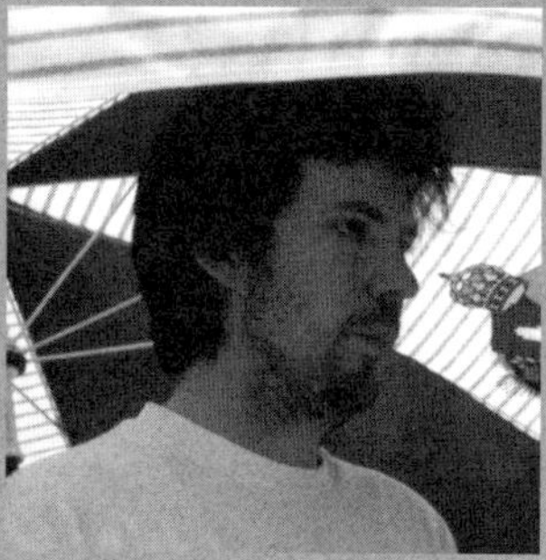

Koen Brams

Debate III

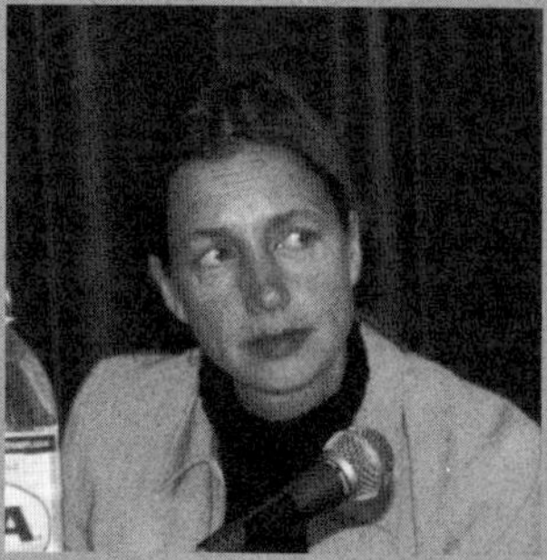

Iwona Blazwick

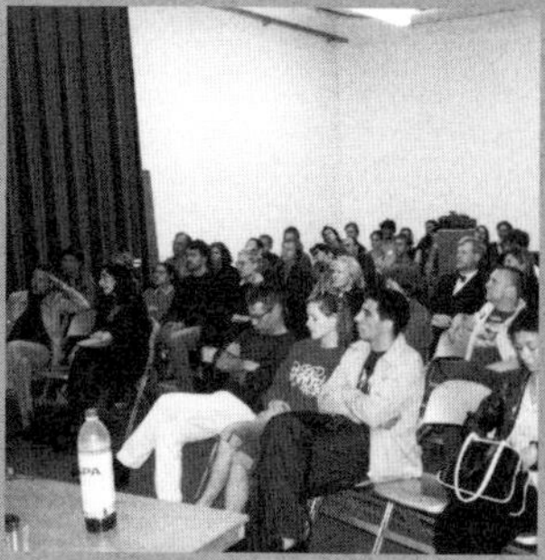

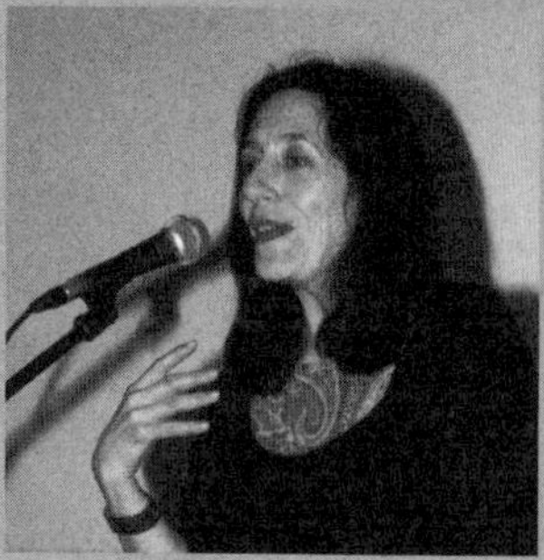

Catherine David

Debate IV

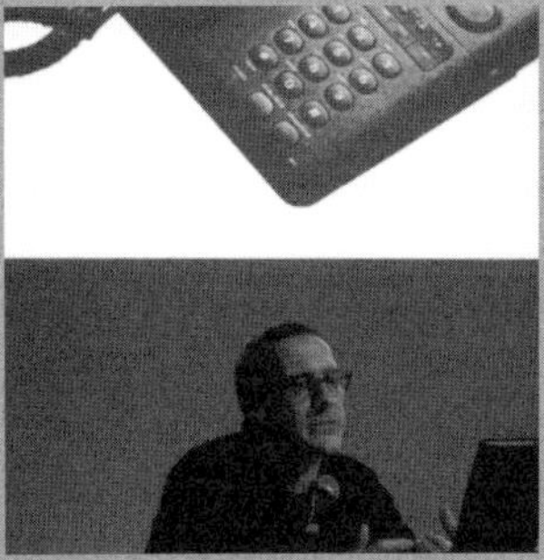

Anthony Dunne

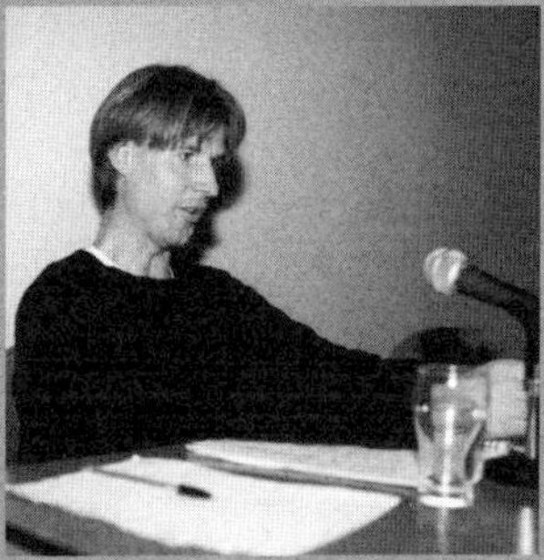

Alan Murray

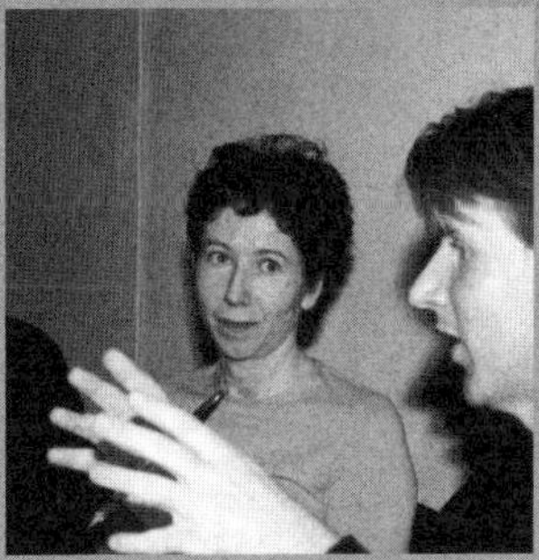

Fiona Raby

Debate V

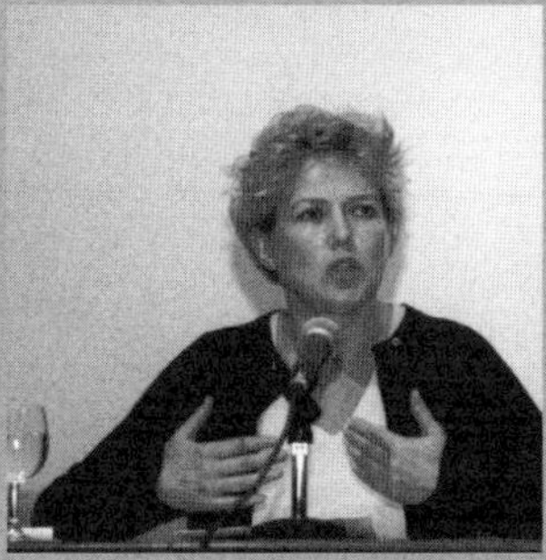

Janneke Wesseling

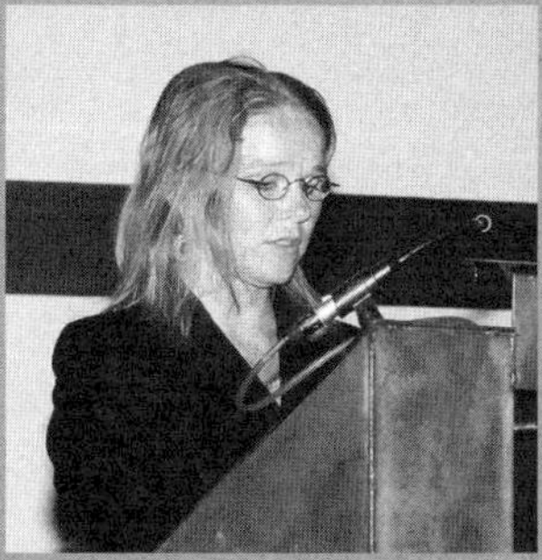

Els van der Plas

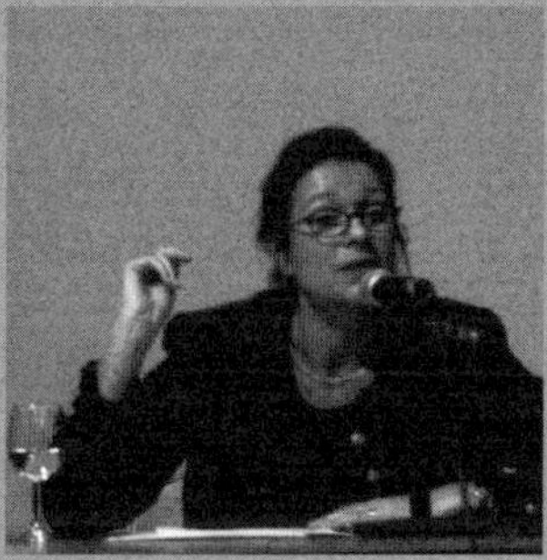

Charlotte Huygens

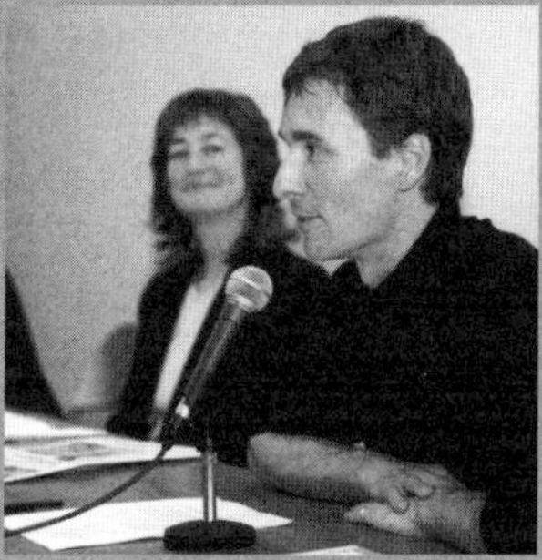

Valentijn Byvanck

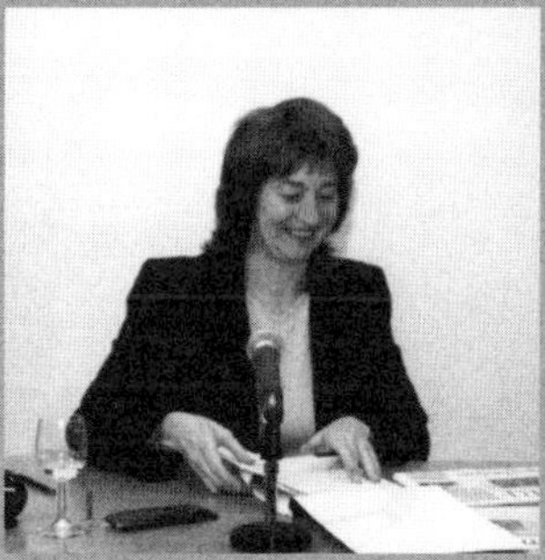

Kitty Zijlmans

I. Art in Public Space

Camiel van Winkel

Bart Lootsma

Siebe Thissen

Foreword

The art world, politicians, and even the public often favor the street, the neighborhood, the traffic square, and the city park over the exhibition space. Art in public space has an undeniably democratic aura; it is more accessible than art exhibited in a museum or a gallery, and from this fact it derives a social status that other art lacks. It has become an established genre with its own institutions, committees, artists and sometimes even with its own idiom. Indeed, the concept of art in public space has become a commonplace, employed by everyone, and not always with stimulating results.

A standard component of the genre is a marriage of convenience with municipal politics. Civil servants and city councilors create conditions for art in public space, write policy documents, set up committees and earmark tax moneys for it. The critic Camiel van Winkel's book *Moderne Leegte. Over kunst en openbaarheid* [Modern Emptiness: About Art and Publicness] describes the ways in which policies have been formulated and implemented over the past fifty years.[1] His study ends with a scathing criticism of today's cultural policy, which in his opinion is based on welfare ideals long since obsolete.

The purpose of the debate in Witte de With was to sharpen a number of viewpoints on the subject. Van Winkel posited that, contrary to the wishes and ideas of artists and officials, public space is not an alternative to, but an extension of, exhibition space. Architecture historian and critic Bart Lootsma explored the consequences of the increasing tendency among citizens and the authorities to withdraw from public space, thus prompting the question what the term public in reference to space or the art shown in it really means.

The debate, entitled *Art on Location*, took place on February 22, 2001. It was organized in reference to the large quantity of public art projects organized in connection with Rotterdam's status as Cultural Capital of Europe that year. The third speaker of this evening was the philosopher and cultural historian Siebe Thissen, head of art & public space at Rotterdam's Centre for the Arts. The city of Rotterdam has asked Thissen to make an inventory of public arts projects to serve as basis for a new policy plan for the arts. He decided not to publish the text of his presentation.

1. Camiel van Winkel, *Moderne Leegte. Over kunst en openbaarheid* (Nijmegen: SUN, 1999).

Camiel van Winkel

Publicness and Recognizability

"Art may gain in meaning by leaving the museum," stated Hans van Houwelingen in an interview five years ago. These days more and more artists are embracing the idea that art would obtain extra relevance – especially in a social sense – if it abandoned its institutions. The number of artists that set up projects in public space or put themselves up for commissions is still growing. They hope or rather believe that in this way the isolated position of visual art will come to an end. Working outside the boundaries of museums and galleries, interacting and communicating with "ordinary people" in places where they live and work would end the socially trivial effects of the professional activities in the art world. At last the indifference of the larger public to contemporary art would be broken. Artists move into city districts to do meaningful and positive things, to contribute to "the quality of public space." According to Hans van Houwelingen: "Artists can increase people's awareness, or they can be an important factor in generating a more livable environment."

Without further ado I would like to make my own statement: There is no fundamental difference between the space of the museum and public space. The museum is merely the culmination of the public realm to which artists are tied, whether they like it or not. I strongly disagree with the popular opinion that art would gain in importance if it withdrew from the museum. I disagree with the opinion that artists could work outside the art context anyway. Art, by definition, always derives its meaning from the art context. All artists, even beginners, work for the museum, whether they wish to or not.

In the past 150 years the necessary connection between visual art and specific techniques, like painting and sculpture, has gradually, however irrevocably, broken off. Anything, literally anything, could be a work of art: any object, any process, any event. There are no more rules or demands that have to be met if something is to be accepted as a work of art. This is a crucial part of the cultural legacy of the avant-garde. Anything could be a work of art, provided there is an artist who designates it as such; an artist who claims: "This is a work of art," and subsequently presents the object, process or event of his or her choice to the public for assessment. The public must be enabled either to confirm or reject the artist's claim: Yes, this is a work of art, or, no, this is not a work of art at all. A work of art does not exist when it has not been brought to the public's attention in the first place, when it has not been "publicized." And why not? Because the lack of rules and demands means that there are no obvious signs left that make a work of art identifiable as such.

Suppose you were walking through a shopping street in a given town and you would notice a heap of sand into which a red pole was stuck. How could you be sure that this was not part of some art project or outdoor sculpture show? I have seen cases that were more absurd. So to be effective as a work of art, the work must be labeled as one, otherwise it remains unnoticed: even if you fell flat on your face onto that heap of sand, you would never guess that it was a work of art.

Visual art derives its meaning from the art context, for every work of art is positioned in relation to other works as well as to texts, theories and concepts that together constitute the art discourse. As a whole, this collection forms a kind of "virtual" or imaginary museum, which is not tied to a place or building. Art magazines and exhibition catalogues are, for example, an essential part of this virtual museum.

It is an illusion to think that it would be possible for an artist to escape from the virtual museum. Of course, artists are able to work in streets and squares, in deserted railway tunnels, at people's homes, in airports, on the beach or wherever; but if they fail to reach the virtual museum – one way or the other, even a small article in *Flash Art* would do – their work remains unknown as a work of art, and is doomed to insignificance.

I repeat my previous statement: There is no fundamental difference between the space of the museum and public space. At this point though, I would like to add that there are nevertheless some differences of degree between the space inside the museum and public space. Saying that these differences are qualifying rather than fundamental, I mean that they basically do not alter the inescapable condition of the virtual museum. I will name three of these differences.

The first difference. In museums and other established art institutes publicness manifests itself as a closed quality. This kind of publicness is characterized by preservation and documentation, by a stable hierarchy. It orders and is cumulative by nature. Everything that takes place in here is being documented and archived according to standard procedures. However, in urban areas outside the museum building publicness manifests itself as an open quality. This second kind of publicness is characterized by the absence of an established memory or self-image; it is unstable, inconsistent and nonhierarchical. The movement of traffic, changes in architecture, the cutting down or planting of trees, coincidental meetings that take place or appointments that are missed; all these events are passing by unrecorded.

Many artists and curators are fascinated with this open quality, and claim that they can appropriate it. Let me give an example. In 1996 the German artist Andreas Slominski put a bicycle tire around a lamppost in the city of Münster. He did not just throw the tire over the lamppost, but had arranged that local authorities assisted him with an excavator and a crane. The lamppost was dug up, disconnected from the electricity supply and lifted from the earth, allowing the artist to place his tire around it. After this, the post was put back, the hole refilled with earth, and all traces of the intervention were neatly removed. The sight of the bicycle tire around the lamppost did not give any reason to assume that it was a work of art. Probably you all have seen a bicycle tire around a lamppost before, or perhaps even thrown one around it yourself. However, the artist took photographs of the event and published them in a catalogue, affirming its art status after all.

For the past fifteen years artists have made many works of this kind within the scope of temporary art events in public space all over Europe, arranging ordinary objects in ordinary, urban surroundings, only having visitors experience the work in the urban context as a work of art via the museum context. With flyers, guides and maps in their hands they are led to appointed sites to undergo a pre-decided, ready-made experience.

In fact what happens is that publicness as an open quality is put on top of publicness as a closed quality. This is the major problem of context-related art events in public space. The public space of the city is subjected to the public space of the museum. Artists and curators flirt with the inconsistent and incomplete power of cognition, which is a property of urban publicness, without giving up – or without being able to give up – their dependence on a museological system of documentation. In other words, the claim to publicness as an open quality cannot be substantiated, with the result that these works of art are leading a totally academic existence.

With that, we arrive at the second difference of degree between museum art and public art. Every contemporary work of art is, fundamentally, a material as well as a conceptual entity. The work of art is a thing, but the thing is also a work of art. The bicycle tire around the lamppost in Münster is an art work that relates to specific ideas about art and refers to other works. Yet it is also a bicycle tire around a lamppost on which your foot is caught if you do not watch your step. A work of art always relates to two kinds of contexts: the spatial context – that is, the direct, physical surroundings – and the art context. These two worlds never coincide; there is a wide gap between them.

This principle applies to any modern or contemporary work of art, including museum pieces. Just think of Joseph Beuys' *Fettecke* (Corner of Fat) – a well-known example, which over keen cleaners mistakenly rubbed off during a museum exhibition. Still inside the museum the label, "this is a work of art," is almost a standard implication. In other words, the gap between the material and the ideal dimension is much wider outside the museum than inside. As I was saying, this is not an absolute difference but a difference of degree.

Contemporary artists working in public space often make the mistake to overlook the gap between these two dimensions of the work of art. They assume that anyone will be able to notice and experience – without the slightest knowledge beforehand – the rhetorical effects through which they have their work inserted into the discourse of contemporary art. They think that the impact of the material presence of the work in public space automatically equals its impact in the art discourse. And then they often add: I don't care whether you call it art or not.

Artists who say about their work, I don't care whether you call it art or not, deny the greatest achievement of twentieth century art: the fact that anything could be a work of art on the condition that there is an artist who has classified it as such and who has presented it to the public as a work of art. The statement, "this is a work of art," is essential for the production and reception of visual art. There is no return possible to the situation in which a work of art entailed a natural unity of form, function and meaning. Anyone who insists that this is still an option, celebrates a state of regression. Artists are able to give up anything but the right to label something, whatever, as a work of art. After all, exercising this right is the only thing that qualifies them as artists.

Before I discuss the third difference of degree, I would like to raise a question. Why is it that artists should play a role in public space? Are there any grounds for the conviction that public art is so important? The question may seem very simple, yet is rarely seriously asked. This is remarkable, because the high expectations that people have of the application of visual art are anything but obvious. These expectations are preferably expressed through the explicit proposition that visual art is actually capable of achieving something. For instance it is said that: visual art can contribute to the quality of public space, visual art can make people more aware of their environment, visual art can enhance the quality of life in town districts, visual art can stimulate social cohesion, visual art can create possibilities for orientation and identification. The question is: what do these statements actually mean? They are suggesting two things: first, that visual art should be considered a form of expertise, and second, that an external appeal to this expertise is possible at any time. We are supposed to believe that artists have capacities that other people do not have, and that these specific abilities add up to the core of their artistic discipline, distinguishing visual art from other disciplines. Furthermore, the suggestion runs that the expertise of the artist should be taken for granted – that it is a general value which is not really under discussion.

The problem is that in reality visual art has lost its basis of expertise quite some time ago; visual art no longer represents a general expertise that artists can collectively refer to. The situation in which artists find themselves today – with an unlimited freedom to choose and handle their material – is at odds with every notion of skill and métier. As I said before, there are no longer any rules that prescribe which technical and esthetic demands an object should meet to be acceptable as a work of art. The regulations and conventions that formerly gave the artists' activities the status of a métier no longer exist. One does not need to have specific skills to be an artist. In essence, visual art does not even need to have a visual character. What visual art is remains an open question; any work of art is a single, particular response to that question.

Even so, just as in the seventies the idea is advocated that artists should be included in urban development project teams to think about life in future cities or to participate in planning new quarters, as if nothing has happened. To underpin this idea it is often suggested that the expertise of artists consist of their "visual and conceptual training," their "spatial intelligence" or even their "social competence." Obviously this is an attempt to reverse the irreversible. Such presumptions are not only regressive, vague and fashionable, but also quite opportunistic, as they suggest that architects, urban planners and urban developers do not, or not sufficiently, have these abilities.

The fact that visual art as a discipline does not any longer represent a general expertise – again, this is not a loss but an achievement – implicates that there are no objectifiable arguments in favor of the contribution of visual art to public space; there are only individual motivations to believe in this contribution. The question of the cultural and social relevance of public art is basically a matter of belief, comparable to the question of the existence of God: some believe in it, others do not. Anyone who asks for arguments gets an individual confession of faith for an answer, which differs from person to person and lacks general legitimacy, since it is impossible to specify in general terms what visual art is, not to mention what it could do.

Why would an individual confession of faith not be sufficient to legitimize the application of visual art? The answer is simple: because one cannot base a policy on this. If you are thinking about public art you have to confront the phenomenon of art policy, for in public space any individual art production will necessarily be preceded by the administrative planning of a commission policy. In contrast with so-called autonomous works of art, any public work of art expresses by definition some form of art policy, be it municipal, provincial, or state policy.

This is the third difference of degree between art inside the museum and art in public space outside the museum. It is primarily a social difference. Every public work of art may be considered an expression – or perhaps a symptom – of art policy. Such an embedment in policy explains why again and again attempts are made to articulate the expertise of visual art in general terms. Public servants, politicians and their advisers have to legitimize financial expenses for art commissions, like any other spending from public funds. Not only the eagerness of artists but also the eagerness of those in charge triggered the public art boom of the nineties.

The Dutch Secretary for Culture, Rick van der Ploeg, gives high priority to art in public space. He considers public art a suitable policy instrument for healing the breach between art and the people, as it was seen in the seventies too. By stimulating public art he believes that the ivory tower in which the professional elite has locked up art can be broken down.

In a recent lecture Thije Adams, a high official in the Department of Van der Ploeg, answered the question why public art was so important. His answer boiled down to one argument: because in this way art could become communal property again. His story was exceptionally rhetorical. First, Adams argued that art in general is not communal property. To prove this he used strictly economic arguments. Then on behalf of the Secretary he dictated the political conditions on which art could and might become communal property again. He was steering towards a conditional subsidy. His reasoning was as follows: the government subsidizes art to serve public interests, so the government can only subsidize those works of art that are in the interest of the public indeed. Accordingly, he concluded that artists must abide by the unwritten rules of public space; their work should be convenient and attractive, open and particularly not confronting. That is what Adams literally said: convenient, attractive and not confronting. From this official's point of view, users and local residents would automatically appreciate works of art if these requirements were met. As a matter of course vandalism of artworks would disappear. It was as simple as that.

Perhaps you are surprised to hear that such ideas circulate inside the Department of Culture in the Netherlands; perhaps you are not. The artists who attended the lecture seemed not surprised. Remarkably, nobody protested against this decree. Apparently artists have accepted the conditions that politicians impose upon their participation. Benefiting from the wishful thinking of politics in an opportunistic manner, they threaten to be reduced to the decorators of consensus society. Politics dictate that the artist please the people, and the artist says: Okay, when can I start?

So much for national politics. On a local level similar ideas prevail. In many large and smaller municipalities the interest in the application of visual art in public space is anything but neutral. Municipalities are competing for the most attractive environment to citizens as well as the most favorable climate to new business activities. Major financial interests are at stake. Local authorities are at pains to highlight the "unique" character of their cities, implementing visual art to give a cultural touch to the marketing of the city.

The funny thing is that by emphasizing local differences all these cities act very similar. In order to realize a "particularization of public space" local authorities from north to south appeal to the potential of visual art. Everywhere it is decided to integrate visual art into architecture and town planning, and to have artists involved in developments as early as possible, although similar concepts extensively explored in the seventies did not work out very well. In most cities the same ambitions concerning public space are heard: to enhance the quality of life, invest in the quality of environments, facilitate orientation and identification, establish the identity of a town district, et cetera.

In fact this is a bizarre, ideologic mix of outdated welfarese from the seventies and well-worn marketing clichés from the nineties: on the one hand the antique, behavioristic notion that monotonous surroundings would lead to "sensory deprivation," alienation and reduction of the "orientation stimulus" in the brains; and on the other hand the worn-out jargon of customer relations, image building and product placement. The shortcomings of the one ideology are used to disguise the weaknesses of the other.

Local governments go for one thing only, and that is recognizability; the recognizablility of their own city or town. And this by means of visual art – of all mediums a medium unfit to strengthen the recognizability of anything, as it is in essence unrecognizable itself. In the policy of these cities identity is reduced to image for the sake of the widest possible recognizability. They fool themselves with a polished-up reputation from which all unwelcome stains were removed, easy to handle as an image, like the logo on the municipal's writing-paper.

The keenness with which many cities have embraced visual art is not incidental; it fits in the excessive fixation on "visual quality" that characterizes the Dutch government's policy concerning spatial planning, urban development and public space. For example, the most important fault of the new Vinex housing estates, which are being built all over the country, is that they have been planned as hermetic compositions, leaving no room to anticipate future developments. Vinex urbanization depends on design and a tempting surface, while it mostly lacks an integrated, regional planning.

The relentless pursuit of visual quality compensates for a general loss of directional instruments and regulatory bodies due to government policy. As a result of cut-backs in public spending, the dismantling of municipal services and an overwhelming emphasis on "more free market, less government interference," the Dutch have created a situation in which commercial companies can determine the priorities of urban planning. This happened in particular Vinex locations where desired varieties and differentiations in the building plan were restricted under pressure from property developers; but it also happened in Amsterdam where local authorities had to resign themselves to the wishes of the business community to develop the Zuidasarea, instead of the banks of the river IJ, into a location of prestigious office buildings.

As soon as the creeping privatization of urban planning liaises with the creeping privatization of public space, for example in the newer generation of shopping malls, the government definitively compromises its credibility on the subject of expressing and protecting public interests. The aim of the current fixation on visual quality in public space is to conceal such a political bankruptcy. The rhetoric of maintaining esthetic standards should reassure us that the government has never lost its grip on developments in the public domain. Visual art appears to be most opportune.

Of course it is a cold fact that a clear, collective outlook on life as well as widely common standards of morality, which the government could smoothly appeal to on behalf of all citizens, no longer exist. However, the way in which this ideologic vacuum is dealt with comes down to a falsification of political discourse. And this is exactly what visual art in public space is used for. The "individual statement" the artist is allowed to make within strictly limited conditions is meant to conceal the lack of an evident set of values in the public domain. The social responsibility of the government is farmed out to a person who could – so we are supposed to believe – do the wonders that ordinary mortals cannot do, such as making people aware of their surroundings, and contributing to the creation of a more livable environment – issues that only two or three decades ago were considered government duties.

Visual art is used as a stopgap measure to mend holes in the connective tissue of the welfare state. Public works of art serve as fig leaves and sops, camouflaging political incompetence and the sell-off of the public domain. Common moral standards and shared principles of life, which over the past fifty years have been dismissed and buried at the graveyard piece by piece, are dug up again and placed as carnival-like zombies in squares and roundabouts.

How pessimistic should we be? Are there any prospects left? Which recommendations can be made to turn the tide? There are two recommendations I would like to make.

First, it is essential that artists and their lobbyists admit that visual art does not stand for a specialized expertise they can take for granted and fall back on. If that has taken place, at least the discussion will reach a higher level.

The second step would be to investigate the relationship between this disciplinary vacuum and the political-administrative vacuum in the public domain. Then artists may start to look for possibilities to make this relationship productive in some way. The outcome of such an undertaking is still a long way off. The only thing we can be sure of is that there will be no room left for naivety and opportunism.

Bart Lootsma

Against (the Overestimation of) Nature

Three years ago I saw an exhibition at the Fondation Cartier in Paris called *Être Nature.* One of its points of departure was French philosopher Gilles Deleuze's proposition that art and culture really begin in nature by demarcating an area and symbolically giving it form. In *Être Nature* the artist Hubert Duprat presented a project involving the larva of the caddis fly, which fashions its fragile brown sheath from grains of sand and scraps of shells, held together with their own saliva. Duprat had placed the flies in an aquarium, but instead of sand he gave them tiny fragments of gold, gems and mother-of-pearl to work with. The sheaths they produced were like beautiful jewelry. The piece consisted of an aquarium in which the insects were at work, empty sheaths and a video of their activities entitled *L'éducation des trichoptères,* the education of the caddis flies. At first sight the piece suggests that much of the quality of art and the built environment simply develops from the context in which it is made and from the way humans and animals approach it. The situation is of course more ambiguous, for the caddis-flies are unaware of the fact that they are making art – it is Duprat who makes art; so does the museum and so do we. Something about the project moreover suggests that humans and animals just do make more beautiful things in a richer environment. I hope it was meant in a naive, ironic way.

In a certain sense – and within limits – it's easier for animals to adapt to their environment than people. Animals rely on their own instinct and act accordingly. Humans lack this instinct. Our bodies, unfit to adapt to the environment by making a minor adjustment, are forced to change that environment by means of culture, writes Scott Lash.[1] By means of culture, of language, we transform our natural surroundings. Our bodies suffer from another defect too: we are vulnerable to the ravages of our environment. We create "worlds" in order to compensate for that defect but (because instincts cannot compensate) our bodies remain vulnerable and suffer pain because of those selfsame worlds.

1. Scott Lash, *Another Modernity, A Different Rationality* (Oxford/Malden (Mass.): Blackwell Publishers, 1999).

Sadly touching in this context was what a rich textile merchant had to say in the television program *The Leisure Society* (VPRO television, 2001). Sick of Rotterdam's urban grimness, he and his wife had built their own Eden in the province of Zeeland. His wife dabbled in something that resembled art and that she undoubtedly thought *was* art. Anyway, she was enjoying herself with color and material. But the day would come, the man realized, when his children would have to leave home to go to college. As a means of accustoming his son to the perils of the big city, the father would occasionally take him to town in his four-wheel drive. The experiment does not seem to have been very beneficial though, for in the boy's eyes anyone simply waiting for a bus was a potential criminal.

External and internal influences have wrought drastic changes on society over the past two decades. The full extent of the consequences of globalization and individualization is becoming apparent. No longer just in the big cities but, due to the influence of international media networks and greatly increased individual mobility, literally everywhere. The city is no longer synonymous with the physical manifestation of one community with a lucid – preferably hierarchical – structure. This also means that the structure of society can no longer be directly deduced from a city's morphological structure; a city is not just an accumulation of similar entities. I use the word "city" here in the extended sense of an urbanized area. Numerous smaller and larger communities find a place in this widespread, almost unlimited area in ever-changing constellations, side-by-side and pell-mell, the communities no longer defined by their permanent physical proximity in a limited territory. To a growing extent communities are being formed by active, deliberate choice and proximity in terms of time-spans. This goes further than clammy blanket designations of what is referred to as "multicultural society" which, however nicely formulated and well meant, almost invariably begins as an invasion of strangers from somewhere else. And that is only one aspect of the matter. Landscape architect Adriaan Geuze, in his account of the residential history of the Maaskant apartment building in Rotterdam, shows that there is a vast difference in homogeneity and community feeling between the building's original and new residents.[2] Not people from other countries, mind you, but simply (in this case younger) people with far more individual lifestyles.

Sociologists like Ulrich Beck and Anthony Giddens see individualization as an unavoidable and necessary intermediate stage on the way to new social forms. In classic industrial society there was a direct connection between class, family, sexual role-patterns, the division of labor between men and women, marriage and architectural typologies. Now, though, many more people have the opportunity or are forced to replace the standard biography by a biography of their choice: a "do-it-yourself biography" as Ronald Hitzler calls it, or, in Giddens' terminology, a "reflexive biography."[3] According to Ulrich Beck, individualization duly means "first, the disembedding and, second, the re-embedding of industrial society's ways of life by new ones. In which the individuals must produce, stage and cobble together their biographies themselves."[4] The reflexive element in this case is confrontation and interaction with the other. This will obviously play a crucial role when people live increasingly closer together, a situation which in the United States – the nation that strongly advocated liberal individualism during the Cold War and still does – has never manifested itself so strongly as in South America, Asia, Europe or the Netherlands. There was always room for expansion in America, and there was always a new frontier.

All this turns culture in the widest sense of the word upside-down, particularly when we are dealing with aspects of culture that appear in public space and derive their legitimacy from their public status, such as architecture and the visual arts. Architecture does after all traditionally mediate between the individual wishes of the commissioning agent and the interests of the public. The architect gets paid by this agent, but also has to convince him of the limits the public sets to his wishes. Art in public places traditionally produces the kind of symbols in which a society can recognize itself. Even when art was a highly individual expression of its maker, it was always legitimized by the artist's special status and gifts. Architecture and art were legitimized by a discourse on *art* and *architecture* – albeit a constantly changing discourse, and imposed from above by *culture*.

2. Adriaan Geuze, "Onze Flat," *Jaarverslag Stimuleringsfonds 1994* (Rotterdam: 1995).
3. Ulrich Beck, "The Reinvention of Politics: Towards a Theory of Reflexive Modernization," in: Ulrich Beck, Anthony Giddens and Scott Lash, *Reflexive Modernization, Politics, Tradition and Aesthetics in the Modern Social Order* (Cambridge/Oxford: Polity Press/Blackwell, 1994).
4. Ibid.

During the period of postwar reconstruction *Openbaar Kunstbezit* [art for the public] – a radio program broadcast weekly on one of the two Dutch stations – and museum education both played vital roles in teaching the public to understand this art. I suppose most people's parents still have the familiar black and pale blue loose-leaf folders on their bookshelves. Until well into the eighties *Kunstschrift* was the art magazine with the largest circulation in the world. Flushed with victory, the social democrats thought that if a magazine enjoyed such a huge circulation it must surely be commercially viable. *Openbaar Kunstbezit* established itself in the former Vondel Church in Amsterdam and rapidly bought up a succession of limping cultural journals before going bankrupt within two years. With its demise, a large part of Holland's art-propagating infrastructure vanished in one fell swoop.

In the seventies Dutch museums still ran large educational departments which in the case of the Haags Gemeentemuseum actually assumed power. As well as initiating an educational policy designed to teach people what art was all about, the museum presented – and still does – mass culture and individual interiors alongside period rooms. Even in those days the museum's policy was to thematize ethnic and cultural minorities, as in its project on orientalism in art. The Haags Gemeentemuseum's "art-cart" took to the streets with a view to bringing art to the people. The initiative foundered due to the public's hostility towards the cart's "crew," and the standard of the presentations, in an effort to stimulate public interest, sank to such depths that this could scarcely be called art. The kiss of death was administered to this educational policy by Rudy Fuchs, who in Eindhoven's Van Abbe Museum pared down the educational department to a minimum and resurrected a temple of art. People were scandalized, but they were silenced when unprecedented crowds thronged to view Fuchs' elitist *Documenta*. The public was evidently ready for the challenge.

Nowadays we all receive twenty or thirty television stations in our homes, and there are consequently at least as many subcultures. Each of them picks its own program or concocts its own mixture. Six-year-olds choose their own clothes. In culture, education now means learning to choose. Learning to choose in the sense of learning to shop, learning to zap and learning to surf.

I have recently observed that *Openbaar Kunstbezit* and the aforementioned excellent educational policies are all but forgotten, and that urban councils and museums are making inept and naive attempts to set up children's galleries and educational pavilions. But what is currently going on in the Netherlands is a far cry from cultural educational policy: it offers a culturally correct form of leisure activity. To start with, we suddenly have a choice between the Kunsthal and a gallery for the kids, between the Institute of Architecture and the educational pavilion. No attempt is made to integrate educational policy and exhibition making. There is no organic intermingling because they are separated by walls and by roads to be crossed. Children can also choose between the kid's gallery and a skate-park. This is market strategy projected onto the cultural world: a form of target-group mentality and theming without any deeper concept of what culture is, let alone what it should be. There is not a jot of difference between the way a city like Rotterdam offers both a skating rink and a sculpture route, both Schouwburgplein and Museumpark, and the way project developers in Zeeland offer mountaineering and deep-sea diving as well as watercolor classes in *The Leisure Society*. They all cater to the public's "needs." And if they fail to arouse sufficient interest they are simply dropped – something that happens in the cultural sector as well. Not that it really matters whether the market does all this or whether people form their own associations and clubs to make their dreams come true. They are apparently perfectly capable of doing so. But the question is whether the government should be similarly led by supply and demand. Isn't it an essential task of the government to introduce from time to time unpopular measures on the basis of democratic decisions and broad social debates, if this serves the common good? And shouldn't this involve the communication of that greater common good?

The canonization of modern art in the Netherlands after World War Two and the vast quantities in which it has been and still is being installed in public space as a consequence of existing subsidy schemes, has led to a situation in which artworks in most cases have become either inoffensive and bland or downright unwanted. In his book *In Holland staat een huis* (1995), containing a photographic documentation of 120 postwar residential districts, Adriaan Geuze demonstrated that due to the sheer quantity of artworks and their interchangeability, they have virtually lost their meaning.[5] They are no longer perceived as expressions of a common, higher good. This is not only

5. Adriaan Geuze/West 8, *In Holland staat een huis* (Rotterdam: NAi Publishers, 1995).

because artists are still basking in a kind of *Openbaar Kunstbezit* climate, but also because the government no longer provides an image of what society is – or ought to be – that goes any further than incidents and political risk-control. I was a member of the *Beeldende Vormgeving* [visual design] committee in Arnhem when war veterans foiled the placing of a work by Manfried Ortner on John Frost Bridge, declaring the site to be "hallowed ground," and because the artist was in any case an Austrian. One might see the piece's non-installation as a mark of respect for the veterans, but what it really boiled down to was a specific group's privatization of a piece of public space. On the other hand, the councilor for cultural affairs – a member of the democratic D66 party – held that all artworks offered to the city by individuals and organizations should by that token be accepted on the envisaged site. The result was a spate of bronzes like *Arnhemse Meisje* [Arnhem Girl] and a head of Audrey Hepburn, which because of the makers' copyright on art on crucial sites in the city precludes any chance of ever installing any other works there. I resigned. As a token of esteem for doing so, I was invited back to sit on the committee in charge of the external appearance of buildings, where I am currently involved in a similar process. Read Kees Christiaanse's column in the next issue of *Archis* – it's about Arnhem.[6]

Although this situation has become more evident over the past ten years, what we have here is of course a development which has been going on for a long time and which has to do with the increasing democratization of society. The French nobleman Alexis de Tocqueville, who visited the United States on a study-trip in 1831, already observed that the urge to create splendid monuments was diminishing under the influence of American democracy.[7] He did however point out that this did not reflect the standard of culture. If the Romans had known more about the laws of hydraulics they would never have built the aqueducts surrounding the ruins of their towns but would have put their power and wealth to better use. If they had invented the steam engine perhaps they might not have built those long, artificial communication routes known to us as the Roman roads. These things are splendid memorials to both their ignorance and their greatness. A nation that leaves no traces except a few lead pipes in the soil and a few iron girders

6. Kees Christiaanse, "Dudok. Extracts from a supervisor's diary," *Archis*, no. 1 (2001): 69-70.

7. Alexis de Tocqueville, *Democracy in America*, vol. 2 (New York: Vintage Books, 1990).

on its surface might well master nature more effectively than the Romans did. The leveling of science, literature and art, according to Tocqueville, was less a sign of indifference than a logical outcome of the disappearance of class distinctions and the dynamic process in which people of different status associated with one another and imitated and influenced one another. These days it is advertising, fashion and popular culture that play this role to perfection.

New ways and means must be explored in order to define how culture could manifest itself in the urban situation. The mechanisms governing urban planning, architecture and art in public space are taken for granted, and deserve to be discussed. Now that modern art and architecture are so widely accepted that they are almost disregarded, they have lost their emancipatory, utopian strength.

The first major step is to abandon the disciplines' traditional fortresses so as to gain unrestrained access to the desires and potential that are present in society and the built environment, and quite literally to chart them. Only then can subcultures really be taken seriously. The word "subculture" still smacks of a second-rate fringe phenomenon, but this qualification is gradually becoming untenable. I should like subculture to be seen more in analogy to what Ulrich Beck calls "sub-politics," by which he means a kind of politics in which society is built up from the bottom. This kind of politics is certainly in the prosperous welfare states of Western Europe a consequence of the advancement of knowledge, increased self-confidence and concomitantly greater independence. Because of this, individuals still communicate with the old institutions but also withdraw from them, "at least when part of their existence is concerned: their identity, their involvement and their courage," states Beck. But: "This withdrawal is not just a withdrawal but at the same time an emigration to new niches of activity and identity."[8]

These niches begin to play a political role at a higher level as soon as they are confronted by the limits of their development. "In sub-politics the political instrument of power is 'congestion' (in both the literal and figurative sense of the word) as the modern form of an involuntary strike," Beck writes. A sign seen by Munich motorists stuck in a traffic jam reads: "You are not in a

8. Ulrich Beck, see note 3.

queue, you are the queue," exemplifying this parallel between strike and congestion. It is a statement perfectly consistent with a comment made by (the entirely unimpeachable) American political scientist Colin Bird. In his book *The Myth of Liberal Individualism* (1999), he claims that Margaret Thatcher's remark "There is no such thing as society," is just as ridiculous as saying that there is no such thing as "traffic," just individual cars.[9]

Of course a number of questions about how Beck's sub-politics is supposed to function go unanswered; in the first place how it is organized and what are its strategic instruments of power. Secondly, it is important to know the background and underlying program of sub-politics, its "secret agenda" if you like, and thirdly, in what form it manifests itself, and in what forums.

At present it looks as though the Netherlands is by no means ready for a debate on this subject, although the television program *De Nieuwe Wereld* occasionally makes an interesting start on an inventory of the problems. The debates on physical planning are the only ones that come anywhere close to the kind of debates Beck means, for it is then that the Dutch are unanimous: when vegetation and open landscape in the country's Green Heart are endangered. This also generates culture in the work of diverse architects and artists including MVRDV and Hans Venhuizen.

However, at the moment the Dutch government is in a phase in which individualization, which since the sixties has been manifesting itself into an inevitable global process, is suddenly being promoted and facilitated with every possible means. The strange thing is that cold-war rhetoric is more rampant at the moment than it ever was during the cold war. If I remember rightly, the social democrat Rick van der Ploeg [Dutch Secretary for Culture] regards Friedrich Hayek's *The Road to Serfdom* (1944) as the most important book he has ever read, despite the fact that this defence of liberal individualism is regarded today in the United States as an excrescence of cold-war propaganda.[10] In the book *Het Wilde Wonen* (1998), which urges us all to go ahead and have a house built by Carel Weeber, Wouter Vanstiphout shamelessly compares the latter with Michael Gorbachev.[11] In *Nederland Regelland* (1999), Lucas Verwey states that government rules are absurd and advises us

9. Colin Bird, *The Myth of Liberal Individualism* (Cambridge/New York: Cambridge University Press, 1999).
10. F.A. Hayek, *The Road to Serfdom* (London/New York: Routledge, 1944/2001).
11. Wouter Vanstiphout, "Naar het Wilde Plannen," in: Carel Weeber, *Het Wilde Wonen* (Rotterdam: Uitgeverij 010, 1998).

to scrap a large number of them as soon as possible. In *Archis,* Camiel van Winkel approvingly describes the illegal parceling in the Leidsche Rijn development scheme as a "rhizome."[12] Artists, planners and architects revel in the first part of Deleuze and Guattari's *Capitalisme et schizophrénie* (1972/1980) without taking the trouble to read the first, highly critical part.[13] By the same token they apparently revel in the literature of Kevin Kelly and his admiration of the self-organizing and self-regulative processes in nature, science and on the Internet. But, as Colin Bird says, a person can claim that society is "organic" or controlled by an "invisible hand" superior to the government, but this has nothing to do with how people behave towards each other in daily life, or ought to. "The simple fact that a jellyfish is organic does not invest the creature with a moral status equal or superior to that which is ascribed to human beings."[14] Conversely, theories like those put forward by Kevin Kelly are not the slightest help to critics in their assessments of plans or artworks.[15] If it is true, as Sanford Kwinter posits, that the entire world and even the cosmos are governed by vibrations like those described in string theory, then that is very interesting from a scientific point of view, but by the same token it applies to everything and thus to every building and every work of art.[16]

What nobody seems to realize is that abolishing rules and laws only creates precedents, encouraging people to take every conflict to court or the media. This is bound to end in a chaotic inequality of justice and even more sticky decision-making. Even artist Joep van Lieshout, who wants to found his own free state with his AVL-Ville, has discovered that it's not that easy to write a constitution that really offers freedom.

Dutch viewers of the Dutch satirical television program *Jiskefet* could recently see how actor Michiel Romeyn reacted to a little orange house being built a hundred yards from his balcony. It suddenly became clear that Romeyn

12. Camiel van Winkel, "'It's fantastic here,' Leidsche Rijn and the bittersweet fruits of Vinex," *Archis,* no. 7 (2000): 30-39.
13. Gilles Deleuze and Félix Guattari, *Capitalisme et schizophrénie,* vol. 1: L'Anti-Oedipe (Paris: Les Editions de Minuit, 1972); *Capitalisme et schizophrénie,* vol. 2: Mille Plateaux (Paris: Les Editions de Minuit, 1980).
14. Kevin Kelly, *Out of Control, The New Biology of Machines, Social Systems and the Economic World* (Reading (Mass.): Addison-Wesley Publishing Company, 1994).
15. Colin Bird, see note 9.
16. Sanford Kwinter, video Berlage Instituut, Amsterdam/Rotterdam, 2000.

never portrays characters in *Jiskefet* but simply plays himself. What emerged even more clearly was that the kind of liberal individualism typical of students and parenthetically propagated in *Jiskefet* results in the opposite of individual freedom. Individuals fall with sentimental pathos into the arms of like-minded groups. And that like-mindedness is mainly apparent in what they all reject. *Not In My Back Yard*. They settle in thematically arranged neighborhoods: near a golf-course, around a swimming-pool, close to a marina or along Amsterdam's ring of canals, and they get rid of everything that doesn't fit in with their surroundings. At this point everyone claims justice: from plebeian computer salesmen to catholics, muslims and art-school students in the category ranging from Michiel Romeyn to Joep van Lieshout. There will certainly be room for some kind of art in these neighborhoods, but not the "art in public space" we are accustomed to talking about as an expression of a common concern or interest. There won't even be any more public space by then, and art will have to adapt to strictly thematic rules like those laid down by commerce. Atelier van Lieshout is a business, not a state.

Jiskefet, that is Dutch culture today, with a Secretary for Culture who thinks it's fun to announce at a meeting that he's off to blow-dry his hemorrhoids.

If I remember rightly, one of former prime minister Joop den Uyl's election slogans was that every worker ought to have his own car, Wim Kok wanted every worker to share in industry's capital gain, Adri Duyvestein now wants to give every worker a house and as far as Rick van der Ploeg is concerned, every worker deserves his own artwork. Their successors will undoubtedly promise every worker his own slave. As a matter of fact the slaves are already there – in Asia, in India and in Africa, but that won't prevent the Dutch Labor Party from stating the claim anyhow. I look forward to seeing how those slaves will reorganize themselves into unions, political parties, residents' associations, the labor press and art for the public. How they will build up a new culture in which art will be able to come out of the closet again into public space. But we shall have to wait a while for that, I fear.

Bart Lootsma, Siebe Thissen and Camiel van Winkel

Debate

Valentijn Byvanck

The first question is for Siebe Thissen, who for the center for the visual arts is drawing up an inventory of projects in public space for the Rotterdam municipal council's future policy document. Do you observe municipal and economic interests in the projects you are inventorying?

Siebe Thissen

Yes, of course interests are involved. But there are limits. The speakers today present art as something monolithic, something that is always the same, and the government is the villain of the piece who plays a controlling or coercive role. That's not how I see it, though. People attribute too much power to government, as if there were a rich world of art whose development is hampered by a visual arts policy. But art is created on a vast amount of fronts, and public space as we used to know it is fragmented. The question is: what are the consequences of this for the public aspect – I haven't heard that question here yet. With the loss or privatization of public space, the call for openness in getting louder. The city is turning more and more into a kind of billboard, chatbox or advertising space in which more and more people are expressing themselves more and more specifically. From graffiti to stickers, from radios at open windows – communication is going on all over the place. This afternoon we heard that people who recognize one another's stickers leave messages on them and make contact that way. This is gradually resulting in a maelstrom of signs and images; it's all very much like the way companies, which have annexed public space, present themselves. I find this "logofication" of everything an extremely interesting phenomenon. It enables you to read cities and that can be most informative: for example about how people behave towards each other, and what the network society looks like and what forms it is beginning to assume. That's my personal fascination: the city as a newspaper, which is getting livelier all the time.

Camiel van Winkel

Where does art come into all this?

Siebe Thissen

We all have our personal fascination with art in public space. I think that a whole lot of artists are giving cities a distinctive look. Take Jeroen Jongeleen with his interventions, and Marc Bijl and Stephen Maas in Berlin, who hang their own signs on building sites. The city has become very readable to me. Sometimes it reminds me of the way pygmies read the jungle. It makes us smile, but we are starting to see more clearly what appeals to people in cities, where they hang out.

Bart Lootsma

One question is: what is art, another question is: what is the government's role in that spectrum, or should we just let it all happen?

Siebe Thissen

We shouldn't let it just happen, but we ought to stimulate things which are potentially already there, make them visible without them immediately catering to a market. It's a very difficult task, because you have to keep on learning from developments. I don't think one should formulate a policy precisely in advance. I do think that policy and practice should be much closer together.

Valentijn Byvanck

Isn't that a curious point of departure for drawing up a policy document?

Siebe Thissen

We have this discussion all the time internally. We'd rather be flexible than draw up a policy plan. Cees Weeda, head of the department for Cultural Affairs in Rotterdam, says exactly the same thing. But the minute you call for flexibility you're accused of being arbitrary. It's as if there are two schools of thought in the Rotterdam Municipal Corporation. One of them says we should let things take their course and learn from the city. The other says everything should be formulated and fixed in writing, otherwise we'll end up with a Peperian muddle with the various departments doing their own thing.[1] It is also obvious that the city is much further than we think.

1. A reference to Bram Peper, former mayor of Rotterdam, who by relaxing controls in his departments opened the door to various forms of malpractice.

Everyone complains about policy, as we recently heard in Zaal de Unie in a debate about broad and narrow views of culture.[2] People said it was ridiculous for the government to earmark money for the visual arts and music, which haven't existed as separate categories for ages. But in practice you see that an institution for the visual arts that does get that money won't use it for traditional art projects anyway, and the shift envisaged by the government takes place after all. And so the council allocates budgets to institutions, and inside those institutions you see all sorts of networks in which quite new things germinate.

Camiel van Winkel

But now you are denying the existence of the gigantic institutional network in the Netherlands for art in public space. A huge amount of money is involved there, and I don't see the city of Rotterdam neglecting this trend.

Siebe Thissen

It's not really all that much money in my opinion; I don't know where that story comes from. I believe Vlaardingen gets just as much for public space as Rotterdam. People often talk about the percentage scheme that still operates in Rotterdam – one percent of construction costs to be spent on art – but there is never any notification. The government has to find out for itself, who is building what and then go begging for that measly percentage. In any case, a lot of commissioning bodies have been wanting to abolish the scheme for a long time now because it's too much of a hassle. All that's left is a pittance from the council's urban renewal fund, and that's due to stop in two years' time anyway.

Camiel van Winkel

That's utter nonsense. Every large or small town has a committee and a budget for that kind of thing, commissions are issued and so on. I think more money is involved here than in art museums.

Audience

Why do you think that public space is disappearing?

2. Zaal de Unie, a Rotterdam debating hall.

Siebe Thissen

In our sessions in Zaal de Unie we broached the question: what is public space? Everyone has their own definition: some say it ought to be free, others say it is outdoors, still others say it ought not to be estheticized. The main thing is content. What I'm trying to say is that private and public are closely interwoven and that in some way this has led to a tremendous boom in publicness. In lots of ways. Art is one of the many things that go on in public space. Alongside all those other things, without any hierarchy.

Camiel van Winkel

What a feeble story! After all, you do have a post in policy-making, you do have a responsibility. The artists sitting here simply want to know what their situation is and what commissioning policy is. What are they supposed to make of such a vague tale about learning from the city and flexibilization? They're just terms for processes, nothing else. They don't tell us anything about content. What has come out of the project? Can't you give us some interim conclusions?

Siebe Thissen

Of course I can. We just have to take a look at what it means in practice. And of course a lot of variants are conceivable. Everything I've heard here today is absolutely true. Art in public space is very often an estheticization of public order. Sometimes it is meant to brighten up a particular neighborhood. Even so, I think a lot of artists are showing us something different within the scope of those possibilities.

Audience

Don't the problems encountered by artists in public space apply to the museum situation too? Doesn't the artist depend on the kind of policy that is controlled by all kinds of other interests there as well?

Camiel van Winkel

Of course, but that's a different story. The big difference with art produced in the so-called autonomous circuit – which, incidentally, I am not praising to the skies – is that the latter can be produced without a prior policy. Art in public space, certainly permanent and semi-permanent work, is not produced until there is a policy for it. Contrary to what Siebe Thissen claims, I don't want to abolish that policy; by definition it can't be stopped.

Siebe Thissen

I think that's such an odd distinction. The entire discourse on art is policy-packaged, isn't it? The debate on art in public space applies to all the visual arts.

Camiel van Winkel

And I stated clearly that in that sense the difference between museum space and public space is not fundamental but gradual.

Audience

The fieldwork that has to be done, and also the inventorying of projects, ought to be taken more seriously in the intellectual debate. People tend to poke fun at this work because there are so many snags. But as an artist I need that policy. I want the whole institutional apparatus behind me if I'm to do what I want to do. The fact that the entire apparatus, the funding, enables us to work is of paramount importance, and it has to be controlled properly. Even stupid policy is good enough for that. What we need are policy-makers who, no matter whether it's nonsense or not, can persuade the politicians to believe in the stuff.

Bart Lootsma

That is true. Policy is very important and we are in an art context here, so we have to discuss it. I think it is very interesting that all art produced for public space is regarded as being of equal standing. A bold statement, and one which wouldn't have been made ten years ago. And it certainly ought to be questioned. For example: what is the government's role? Should it stimulate everything? What about neighborhood parties, rappers, billstickers? Do they qualify too, or not quite? Or should one say: it's all happening, that's great, but let the government focus on stimulating things that are not so popular, things that industry won't sponsor. Is the government going to focus on artists and themes, which are not popular, artists who are preoccupied with death for instance; is politics going to fund that kind of art. That's not what I am hearing, and it means that a number of evident choices have already been made.

Siebe Thissen

It is quite possible that with issues like this we are in something of a transitional phase. We are seeing more and more groups in society that want to formulate their own policy. Often policy is automatically controlled by artists who organize themselves. And often not just artists, but a philosopher and an architect, say, who join forces to make art can have the same effect. The system is splintering. Why mightn't it have been replaced by something else in a few years' time?

Camiel van Winkel

Because the system is designed to perpetuate itself. In that sense this policy is certainly an end and not a means, for it is produced by a self-perpetuating machine.

Siebe Thissen

I don't believe a word of it. Take the city of Rotterdam, for example. The city department that used to be responsible for arts policy is now in charge of "cultural affairs," and what used to be the faculty of Art and Culture at Erasmus University is now called "Cultural Studies." One thing is quite clear in policy-making: the word "art" is disappearing, everywhere. Discussions are however continuing in policy-making circles about whether to retain the word "art" or not – and there you have that complexity again, those different layers.

Camiel van Winkel

There are financial issues to consider. It has taken twenty years of economizing to get us where we are now, for public space to be commercialized.

Audience

But isn't that because commerce has simply become more active, proposing themes, and it is up to artists to develop ideas? What have artists and the council to offer in the face of commercialized space?

Siebe Thissen

That is a very good question, and one for which I don't have a snap answer. It would be handy if I could pull a file out of my briefcase and read you something I'd written myself. It would be easy to take an old document and rewrite it with a few modifications, but I'd know exactly what I was doing. The tension is already there – in criticism too. You think you have a kind of fortress from which you can launch criticism, and it's quite normal for people to ask me: where are you coming from? Give us some guidelines.

Camiel van Winkel

And then we're told that anything goes. I still think it's feeble.

Bart Lootsma

That's what worries me about that committee responsible for the external appearance of buildings in Arnhem of which I am a member. Town-planning departments are smaller than they used to be. Today, an office is hired to make an urban plan; the person who makes these plans becomes the supervisor and teams up with a group of developers. Subsequently, the council says: so now we'll draw up a contract and you'll guard over quality. Nobody on the council can offer quality and the supervisors are mobbed by commerce. In the United States, they are ahead of us in privatizing public space. Public space there doesn't belong to a city but is managed by local communities. This has far-reaching consequences, also for art in public space. The residents of those communities demand a specific art for their specific neighborhood. Is that what you want, or should the government manage public space? I'd like to hear an answer to that kind of question. I'd also like to hear the answers to questions including what kind of art the government wants to stimulate, what are they paying for because nothing will happen otherwise, and what things do they simply let happen? These are choices that have to be made.

Siebe Thissen

Policy must offer a framework in which artists and groups can place their own accents and be given the scope to make a variety of things possible. That doesn't mean that policy is implemented in accordance with how it is written.

Valentijn Byvanck

But protection is the important thing here, isn't it? Not to dictate but to protect. We live in a society with all kinds of interests, some which are perhaps weaker than others and ought to be government-protected. At any rate, this is one view on what the government can do. But we shall have to continue our discussion about that some other time.

II. Art and Theory

Jeroen Boomgaard

Koen Brams

Foreword

Opinions about the function and significance of theory for art differ widely in the Netherlands. Oddly enough, this has not generated a lively critical tradition. On the contrary, one must search long and hard for theoretical reflection in art institutions, art journals and even in academia. Indeed, some curators and artists heartily detest theory. Even so, few of them would deny the need to reflect on the visual arts. But what is the significance of such reflection for art? How can it add anything to the production or experience of art? And at what point does it become significant for an artwork?

Prior to this debate the critic Jeroen Boomgaard wrote an essay entitled "New Communication, no Message" for the journal *A-Prior.*[1] In this essay, he declared that art practice is not the sole cause for the gap between practice and theory in the arts, as is often assumed. When critics grumble about the not very conceptual character of today's art and about the tendency to hark back to artists' poses of the sixties and seventies, they are really complaining that artists do not satisfy *their* theoretical wishes. Today's artists, though, have a different agenda which, Boomgaard continued, deserve a different theoretical formulation. In his response Koen Brams, former editor of the journal of art theory *De Witte Raaf*, accused Boomgaard on the one hand of lumping all contemporary art and criticism together, and on the other hand of always keeping out of reach himself. He challenged Boomgaard to show his theoretical colors.

The debate, entitled *Good Art doesn't need Theory?*, took place on May 17, 2001. Boomgaard's essay in *A-Prior* referred to an earlier public debate held by the Association for an Art and Research Center in Brussels on May 3, 2000.[2] Boomgaard and Brams were moderators at this debate. Since Boomgaard's essay triggered the debate at Witte de With, it is reprinted here, preceding Boomgaard's further explanation, Brams' reaction and the debate itself.

1. Jeroen Boomgaard, "New Communication, no Message," *A-Prior*, no. 3-4 (2000-2001): 94-126.

2. The debate in Brussels was prepared in a number of private discussions organized and published in part in *De Witte Raaf* (no. 84: 1-19; no. 85: 5-8). Thanks to Etienne Wynants for his help in unraveling this prelude.

Jeroen Boomgaard

New Communication, no Message[1]

In theoretical terms, art at the present time doesn't have a leg to stand on. This need not be so bad, of course, if art, in a variation on a statement by Barnett Newman, has as little use for theory as a zebra has for zoology. But since contemporary art is once again fiddling at the boundaries of the notion of art, it is conceptual from the very start and needs theory as much as a fish needs water. And, all animal metaphors aside, it is precisely at that point that the trouble starts.

The art of today looks in so many respects like that of the sixties and seventies that a sense of *déjà vu* is unavoidable. The shunning of the term "art," as well as the attempt at escaping from the idea of individual artistry by working collectively with small groups of non-initiates, the production of works of art that appear to want to shirk the definition of what art is, the emphasis on actions or ephemeral products that lend themselves badly to commerce, these are all characteristics of today's art, and it's all been seen before. Of course there are differences: since the final victory of capitalism has been secured, the established economic order is accepted as a given fact, even though the concern for alternative forms of living has not been abandoned. But the most important difference, and this is emphasised ad nauseam, consists in the fact that the great utopia has been replaced by the modest ideal. This very difference, however, indicates that a radical change has taken place in the way that artists think about their work.

No animal can elude classification and this goes even more for art, for, however little interest it may want to show in theory, it is already imprisoned in the cage that makes its existence possible. This dependence on theory becomes clearly visible when attempts are made to change the cage. Duchamp with his ready-mades was the first to trenchantly demonstrate that any reflection about art is preceded by the implicit statement that "this is art," (a conclusion reached in Thierry De Duve's equally trenchant analysis). And when experimental art in the sixties and seventies once again aimed at breaking through the frameworks so as to prepare the transition to social reality, then these experiments could only be sent into the world accompanied by the very same

1. This article was previously published in *A-Prior*, no. 3-4 (2000-2001): 94-126.

statement, “this is art,” even, or rather precisely, when this is not what they are meant to be. Art thus found itself caught in the paradoxical situation that the pursuit of a different role, a new form of consciousness that would no longer have anything to do with the outdated ideals of modernism, and the desire to exchange the safe and exalted space of the museum for a place in the public lived environment, could only be understood as such when one had first accepted that one was dealing with art. This ambiguity, which many artists at the time were undoubtedly aware of, lends the work its utopian character: it prescribes a situation that has not yet been attained. Not least because the artists of this generation frequently took up the pen themselves in order to get round this ambiguity and to provide their work with theory (I'll be coming back to this in detail later), the art produced at this time often looks almost like a manual. How one is meant to deal with the new apparatus in order to get it to work in the right way is explained or demonstrated step by step. A manual that not only had to make it clear what purpose the work had to serve, but also how it should function in the future. The manual was all the more explicit seeing as the corresponding apparatus was only virtually present.

Such a protocol for a potential world is difficult to maintain, of course, when that world is not forthcoming. At the end of the seventies postmodernism drew the consequence from this impossible position. Art was the product of a set of rules and circumstances that made its existence possible. Plans for the future were thus replaced by analyses of the context and a lot of works addressed the exhibition, the museum, the art discourse, the art trade, et cetera. The inescapable conclusion was that art was just as autonomous as a car between Utrecht and Amsterdam during the rush hour. That is to say, confined in its own small cage but part of a permanent and unavoidable flow. The theoretical basis of art changed as a result of this observation. The fundamental premise was no longer that art could change reality, or at least adjust the perception of it favourably, as the avant-gardes of the sixties and seventies had intended. Reflection on the position of art, in a cynical or in a critical sense, was seen as the only possibility. Cynical because art produced in isolation as exception was nevertheless hardly distinguishable from other forms of commodities, critical because art was part of the same field of the production of meaning as other forms of communication and was thus capable of subjecting cultural codes to examination. Art that still thought it could prepare a new world in an avant-garde manner was outdated, naive and even somewhat suspect precisely because it clung to the illusion that art occupied a privileged position.

Rather amazingly, this ideal, although pronounced dead, seems to be experiencing a resurrection these last few years. Once again the borders of art are being questioned and, as though nothing has happened, the transition to everyday reality is also being announced. Such a sudden resurrection is difficult to justify theoretically, but this goes even more so for the way in which the new ideals are being propagated. This time a manual with clear instructions is out of the question. A clear point of view is not announced, a theoretical basis is not laid, and artists behave as though the new society is a fact, as though paradise has been established on earth here and now at one go, so to speak. A paradise, then, especially for art that apparently no longer has to worry about any possible ambiguity. As an integral part of society it thinks it can make a critical or personal contribution to a better world. This combination of impetuosity and overestimation of its powers may well be based on a different role for art, but there does seem to be a painful lack of a cohesive concept.

It is not clear what the reason is for this shaky conceptualism, but one thing is sure and that is that it causes a great deal of irritation. Surprisingly enough, most of the criticism comes this time not from the public, who are not very concerned, or from their representatives in the more traditional art criticism, but precisely from the unsuspected corner of the magazines and their writers who engage with the conditions of art's existence. Unsuspected because it is there that the reconsideration of the framework of art is usually received with open arms, because, in other words, the spirit of time-honored avant-gardism still flits freely around. This openness seems almost completely absent with regard to recent art. In this respect the debates organized by *De Witte Raaf* this spring were revealing and disconcerting. The shades of the debates fluctuated between black and grey. Almost without exception, they saw few prospects: the art world has been irretrievably handed over to commerce and young artists are unable or, what is worse, are unwilling to resist. Apparently everything was better in the past and, in order to underline this nostalgic tone, Daniel Buren was allowed to speak extensively in the same issue. His remark that young people are not turning against their surroundings while the whole thing should actually be demolished, underlined the message of the debates. The final debate in Brussels organized by the same magazine was also somewhat gloomy. The critic present actually didn't even want to concern himself any longer with the new forms of engagement, the artist felt that a lot of work testified to an enormous poverty, but also the two participating curators, who after all devote a lot of time to presenting new work, merely thought that one should offer space to it, but they didn't sound all that enthusiastic. It is striking that the criticism of the feebleness of these neo-neo-avant-gardes is often formulated by, or on the basis of, artists who occupied a prominent place in the more politically involved conceptual art of the seventies and eighties. Buren is one of these showpieces, but American art of the eighties is also often cited as an example of how it actually should be done. Isabelle Graw, the editor of *Texte zur Kunst*, negatively compared the work of Tracey Emin with that of Mary Kelly. Not only did Emin deal again with themes that Kelly had already broached, in particular the emphasis on personal life, but she did it moreover in a way that could not stand in the shadow of what her predecessor had achieved. The question, however, is what Graw sees in Kelly that is missing in Emin. Graw's comments about Kelly's *Post-Partum Document* make it clear what that extra value is. The work can be "received on several levels: as a translation of Lacanian concepts, as an explication of feminist representations of female identity or as a continuation of conceptual systems of recording and classification." It has to be said that Emin's sad remains of a failed life is no match for a work with so many levels.

The most important reproach, and wholly understandable as seen from the viewpoint of these artists, is that the young generation hasn't the faintest idea of previous history. As fresh as they are foolish, they set out on paths that have already been trodden flat. Whereas the artists of the sixties deliberately harked back to the ideas and deeds of dada, for example, contemporary artists present their performances and other interactions with the public as though they have never been shown before. It's certainly exasperating, especially if you've already experienced the foregoing; the feeling of superficial repetition makes an open approach almost impossible. Yet this relationship with the past does deserve a bit more attention. History and historical understanding ultimately became particularly problematic in the eighties. The events themselves seemed to deny any model of logic or linearity. But even without the inexplicable developments in Eastern Europe history was already disposed of in theory as an outmoded concept. And it is partly the consequences of this that the younger generation are dragging along with them. But you can hardly blame them. You can hardly call history an arbitrary construction and at the same time use the reproach of a lack of historical awareness. In order to understand today's art we thus have to look at the framework in which it is created, a framework that is in part formed by the same theory that is now so critical of art. Because of the theory of the end of history every avant-garde ideal was made impossible: a vanguard that comes from nowhere and also has no idea where it is supposed to head for drifts rather aimlessly through the world. Leading on from this idea, the return of avant-garde ideals can only be regarded then as the umpteenth simulation, mere fuel for the energy-wasting engine of the art market. Or, if one does not wish to fall into a similar fatalism, a contemporary avant-garde can only be conceived in the form of a reflection upon the issue of the avant-garde or as a more or less politically correct dialogue with other forms of culture. A repetition of the avant-garde as practice, without any reflection upon its possibilities or impossibilities, is conceptually incomprehensible. This at least is how it is for the theoretical approach that can only read art as a palimpsest.

Apparently, today's art keeps too little to the theoretical framework that has been prepared for it. Something has therefore gone wrong in the relationship between theory and practice, the framework no longer fits around the work, or the work no longer adjusts itself within the frame. And this is happening while not so long ago theory and art seemed to be performing an indefatigable pas de deux. In an almost self-evident way artists from the sixties bid farewell to Newman's judgement and theory, writing about art, became a part of the work. Not so much because the work that they were making needed so much more explanation – you could hardly call it more incomprehensible than the work of Newman – but because things that were self-evident had become a problem for them. Since they wanted their work to be seen differently they themselves had to create the conditions for this. The artists at that time refer in their texts not only to the existing art they are opposed to and to the preceding experiments whose thread they wanted to take up again; the texts also serve as a prelude to art's future function and position, acting so emphatically within history. Texts and works together can easily be read as the above-mentioned manual for a different reality.

The eighties' transition to postmodernism had radical consequences for the relationship between work and theory and for the content of the theory itself. The emphatic reflection upon art's functioning, upon the institutional context and the discourse that determined its life, led to artists such as Mary Kelly starting to consider writing more than ever as an essential part of their work, but also to the work becoming subjected more than ever to the regime of interpretation. If the manual or the index was the textual model accompanying the art of the sixties and seventies, then the purloined letter could be seen as characterising the Eighties. Edgar Allan Poe's story, *The Purloined Letter*, about a stolen letter with incriminating contents which is lost and cannot be found since it lies openly in the most obvious place, was enormously popular because of its theme of absence in presence and the interpretations of it by Lacan and Derrida. The multiple readings of the story repeatedly concentrated on the blind spots in the text, on that which is readable yet is not seen. Hidden meanings were also sought for in the art of that period, but this meaning had more to do with the place of the work of art, its placing in code and context, than with the content. It was not the letter itself that stood at the forefront but the place where and the way in which it was concealed. This semiotically influenced emphasis on such elements as sexuality and intertextuality also had other consequences for the role of theory. The moment artists based themselves on models developed in psychoanalysis and linguistics, they more or less allowed thinking about their work to slip out of their hands. Of course artists from the sixties had also vehemently borrowed from then popular theories like phenomenology and gestalt theory, but both in their writings as well as in their works they seemed to deal with them rather casually. In the eighties theory became more emphatically than ever the framework within which art was able to manifest itself. As Hal Foster remarks in *The Return of the Real*, the theoreticians actually represented the continuation of the avant-gardes from the seventies. This created a situation, however, that went a lot further than the simple statement "this is art." The expression that now preceded everything was rather "this is meaning," and the work of art was no more than a small element in the endless production of meaning that could be revealed by means of theory. It also meant that a work of art, in order to count as critical, should investigate all the different layers that theory was concerned with.

It is precisely this layered legibility that Isabelle Graw finds in Kelly and misses in Emin. The fact that more reflectively focussed art criticism tends to prefer art that employs the same discourse, as itself is very understandable. Critic and artist recognise each other and work on a common project. This discursive project, however, places artists who wish to pursue a different direction in a difficult position. Textual interpretation denies the possibility of autonomy: nothing can escape the cultural codes that regulate interpersonal traffic, art included. Indeed, a new appeal to autonomy can, on the basis of current analyses, only be considered as reactionary. The network of texts about texts also obstructs the resumption of ideals from some time ago. The return of art from the past, such as the return of painting in the eighties, was opposed as sinful regression and hopeless cynicism in the self-critical work of Kelly and associates and the related stand of magazines like *October*. In their eyes, the art of predecessors could only be understood as a dialogue in which work from the past is opened up for the present and made legible again. This opening up is not so much a question of revealing forgotten meaning in an archaeological way, but much more of divulging the contemporary spectator's blind spots. This means that art from a previous period can only be taken up when it becomes involved in the analysis of current cultural production and reception. In this light, the quiet and almost stupid return in contemporary art of procedures and ideas from the sixties could be regarded as an effective strategy for escaping from the linguistic network that encompasses art.

One of the major risks in riting about new tendencies is the inclination to declare failure as success. At the risk of falling into this, I would like to take a closer look at a number of characteristics and at the same time relate them to the expectation that they apparently do not come up to. Recent art is often reproached for looking poor. It has to be said, a lot of work does look rather knocked together, almost casual; videos by young artists are hardly on a par with a clip by Madonna. This miserable quality, however, contrasts poignantly with the splendour, size and perfection of a lot of works from the eighties, which joined battle, often with some success, with the overwhelming production of popular culture in spectacular mega shows. Compared to this, the sight of the rancid remains of the depressing daily life of an artist represents a shock, but also the work of artists who do not appear to have totally withdrawn into the private fantasy of an adolescent's bedroom show characteristics that evoke memories of earlier performances and happenings and the events of Fluxus artists: informally and just for friends and close acquaintances. Yet what I have just said is not totally correct. It suggests too much that recent art turns its back on the world of mass consumption and media entertainment. Nothing is less true; mass culture is not competed with, but sought out in the banality of everyday use: a clip of Madonna in a karaoke café.

Literal insertion into daily life is another point of ceaseless criticism. Once again, however, the problem lies more with the expectation that is frustrated than with the art. With the sixties as an example of failure, the professed integration into everyday reality is relegated to the realm of fantasy. Ultimately, as soon as it is brought into the outside world, the work of art inevitably becomes part of the isolated and protected space of art. Surprisingly enough, artists are reproached on the other hand precisely for not being sufficiently consistent in taking the step to real life outside the institutions of art. Through showing their work in the very place they are trying to escape from, they would be admitting from the start the bankruptcy of their undertaking. These reproaches are shortsighted since they misjudge the double game that is being played in art today. After the power of institutions like the museum and the exhibition was labelled in the eighties as overpowering and was also kept firmly in the saddle by the art production described above, one can hardly expect the art of today to be able to suddenly escape from this in a Houdini-like fashion. On the other hand this does not mean that it should simply bow to this power in order to limit itself to the umpteenth analysis of the unavoidable context of art. By presenting work in several places for diverse audiences, this context is questioned, made visible, but also somewhat put into perspective. The work appears able to lead an existence outside it as well. When the stolen letter is found again it can also be read.

Related to this problem of place is that of audience and communication. The idea of open and unhindered exchange in general, but especially of the artist with his public, which was intensely cherished during the sixties, had fallen considerably into discredit in the eighties. Free communication was considered impossible since the message would never arrive in the way it was intended. Code and context were determinant and reflection about this became an important subject for art. The consequence that can now be drawn, however, is a completely different one: if genuine exchange is not possible, then the artist can just as well make use of the common forms of communication and exploit them in all their superficiality. If every message gets lost somewhere between sender and receiver, you can just as easily choose to dispatch a message to the world without worrying about whether it will be properly understood. If every attempt to reach the public suffocates in the soft cushion of art, then perhaps it is better to aim yourself at your immediate surroundings and to radically forget about reach and effect.

The art of today sends out messages simply because there happens to be an all-powerful network of communication. Artists assume that there is always someone in fact who picks up the signal. A manual is not necessary, everyone can always reach each other via the mobile phone, the letter is found again and is written anew each day in thousands of SMS messages. Perhaps the message is regarded as art, but perhaps not. This mixture of cynicism in principles and idealism in deeds is, I think, what is most difficult for theory to digest. The model of noncommittal in which ideals are implemented almost unassumingly arouses so much irritation because it cannot be traced back to any theoretical basis at all. Lack of insight, lack of political notions, lack of ideas about art's role, lack of a vision of society, all these reproaches merely reveal that what is expected of art is a cohesive story. Having consigned the grand narratives to the scrap heap of history, in order to declare instead multiple reading as the standard, theory desires, or rather demands, that art abides by this critical model. By doing this, art supposedly puts itself out of the game; the actual reason, however, could be that theory has to play on its own.

Art at the moment may be conceptual but it is hardly intellectual. It does not serve as a prelude to a future society, but unleashes its experiments on the here and now for whoever wants them. Content is linked to superficiality, but that does indicate the concept that lies behind it. It is a concept that largely has its origins in the thinking of the eighties, but which, as described above, draws from it opposite conclusions. The analysis that art is produced as a separate domain, but at the same time is inextricably connected with the broad field of culture, leads artists to exploit autonomy and at the same time to announce a merger with everyday reality. The self-evident, hardly theoretically constructed way in which this happens has a number of striking effects. Despite the gloominess of theoretical art criticism, curiosity about the limits of art and of how art functions is greater, and the discussions more intense, than they have been for a long time. The negative reaction is the unintended evidence of this. Although this is the issue at hand, the art of this moment does not play a complex game with the many layers of meaning that are being mixed up. Nothing is revealed and little is explained. As Henk Oosterling writes in *Think Art; Practice in the Art of Today*, these days it's more a question of sensitization than emancipation. In art everything is touched upon and broached, but theory hardly plays a role in this. It is an art that wishes to merge into the diffuse field of social possibilities and, just like the avant-gardes before it, it does this by taking the model of technological culture as its starting point. The statement "this is art" has been replaced by "this is communication." An adequate reaction to this is not the cultural despair and moaning that now appears to be the fashion, but a more far-reaching exploration of this starting point and the consequences it has for the role of art. When it does that, theory no longer has to lament its loss of power, for then it will once again have found art on which to base itself.

Jeroen Boomgaard

Theory Today

Theory is the best thing there is, even if the Dutch don't always seem to believe it. Theory enables us to think about art coherently, to reveal underlying principles, to interpret work in a manner that is not immediately obvious, to establish links with other works outside the historical context or, on the other hand, strictly within it, to suggest a link with other cultural phenomena – you name it. And perhaps that is the problem: everything is theory and theory is everywhere. It may sound exaggerated to you, the wishful thinking of someone who has made theory his profession, but this is not quite the case. Even before the painter takes up his brush, before the video artist aims her video-eye at something, before the performance artist takes the stage – every time they embark on making an artwork – there is theory. I am not saying that these artists have a clear idea of what they are going to do and will keep obediently to a program they have invented. On the contrary, making art is a quest for something of which you don't even know what it is going to look like, that much is clear. Usually, though, an artist does know where to look for it; theory has already demarcated the boundary between what is art and what is not, what the current possibilities are and what is already regarded as *passé*, what ideas, no matter how incipient their crystallization, herald something new. Summing up: before an artist begins, he finds himself in a field of theoretical assumptions of which he need not even be conscious. Indeed, the tendency in the Netherlands often seems to be that he is better off not knowing about them. The fact that we are fortunate in having a separate department for theory at the Jan van Eyck Academy clearly implies that other art academies are doing so little about theory that contemplation is not a standard requirement. You will not be surprised that the conclusion to be drawn from this somewhat exaggerated picture of the state of affairs is that the self-chosen stupidity, to which Dutch art so often seems to profess, is based on theory. The dominant theory here often seems to be that of free expression, the rule that an artist must let everything surge up inside him and emerge to flower *à la* Karel Appel. But everything that seems to bubble up so spontaneously from inside has passed through a sieve of possibilities and is therefore shaped not only by the theory of free expression but also by quite different and often conflicting theories.

This is because no theory ever prescribes how art ought to behave, just as there is no conclusive interpretation that might provide a definitive explanation of a work of art. Possibilities are rife with regard to both production and reception, but they cover only a small part of reality and can only partly lay claim to the truth. Theory, then, cannot be contested by empiricism, by which I mean that every theory about art can always be buttressed by examples but can also always be challenged by works, which do not fit in. This behooves the theorist to be modest but may not prevent him from making statements, raising issues, which profess to apply to a large segment of art, launching ideas that claim to be consistent with the state of affairs. Only under the umbrella of such claims can theory be forced to prove that it is more than mere empty talk, to have an effect. For the latter is often at stake on both the production and the reception side: theory serves as a crowbar, a new theory disrupts rusty assumptions, tells us that we are seeing something quite different from what we have always thought we were seeing, or says on behalf of the artist that art is quite different or is doing something quite different than is generally assumed.

Theory always has a critical component, which does not mean that its effect is always critical. However, a theory can fossilize into dogma. Time was, when the theory of free expression also possessed a liberating impulse and, who knows, may regain possession of that impulse one day. But currently that idea has the effect of a dogma that discourages many young artists from reading, thinking, looking around – in short, from gazing further than their own besmirched navels.

The theorist must therefore always beware of suddenly shifting his position and of imperceptibly turning from a critic into a dogmatist. As a kind of *alter ego* of the artist, the theorist must keep searching for a cohesive idea in that which he does not yet understand, constantly renouncing what he had formulated only yesterday as the new truth. He may not forget that his ideas harbor no more than a possibility and not a final destination and that, just like art itself, he must bear other possibilities in mind.

The moment at which a critical theory exchanges its crowbar function for that of a barrier is hard to determine, however. Not retrospectively, because retrospectively we can all see that silly Clement Greenberg totally misunderstood pop art, that naive Michael Fried failed to realize that high modernism's heyday was over. It was of course not in the least obvious to

Fried and Greenberg themselves, and many of their contemporaries, however willing they were to keep their eyes open for new developments, may have often wondered whether these theorists were not perfectly right after all. It was not that their theory indiscriminately opposed every form of new art; on the contrary, they fervently believed in the innovation of art. However, they felt that art was going downhill at that time, that it no longer satisfied the conditions that art ought to satisfy in their opinion. So all of a sudden they exchanged their vanguard position for the rearguard; their crowbar had become a barrier against other opinions and forms of art. History is full of such almost tragic moments: the same thing happened at the end of the seventies, when neo-Marxist art criticism advocated a critical rapprochement with mass culture, only to be confronted with the return of painting in a manner that made mass culture of it, at the same time appearing to underline art's autonomy again. The rejection of certain forms of postmodern art from this critical leftwing corner is perfectly understandable, for every form of social engagement seemed to have been abandoned, and this approach still exists, witness Hal Foster's *Return of the Real* (1996). At the same time, though, that same rejection precludes any insight into the theory of postmodern art and its inherent possibilities. It would be going too far to embark on a lengthy account of critical theory's struggle with postmodern culture, but the result in the eighties was in any case a theory of art best described as neo-Marxistically colored deconstructivism. I imagine that you are sufficiently familiar with elements of that theory and shall therefore not dwell on the details of cultural, or rather multicultural consciousness, the problem of identity and gender, the problem of art's position as a mass medium and at the same time as a criticism of mass culture, the idea of art's being a specific code and at the same time a reflection on different codes, et cetera. Generally speaking, that theory regards art as part of a more universal visual culture, whereby art can utilize elements from that visual culture, incorporate them, relate to them (advertisement, design, film, television, corporate culture), and on the other hand demands of art a critical reflection which in a certain sense might be termed discursive. In that theory art is supposed to provide an analysis of, for instance, the medium that is used or the position within art as institution, an analysis that can be written out as theory, so to speak. This has produced – and still is producing – a lot of very interesting art, witness recent work by Pierre Huyghe in the Van Abbemuseum.

But meanwhile another kind of art has appeared which treats these principles far too casually, giving rise to a great deal of irritation among theorists. Not a trace of theory can be discerned in this kind of art. Its makers just seem to be carrying on with a curious kind of optimism: as if everything is always possible, as if the world is a vast tabula rasa on which art can think up a new task to perform every day.

For the theorist or critic this kind of art is rather awkward. What can you say about it, for heaven's sake, except that it's all been done before, or that not enough reflection has gone into it? There's little to be said *for* it, unless of course you resort to the same superficiality and ride on the latest modish wave. But what critical theorist in his right mind would want to have that on his conscience?

That's why theory is now in the same position as Greenberg and Fried thirty years ago. The art currently being produced does not tally with what theory would have art be: it simply lacks the right quality. The crowbar of theory is being used as the knife of criticism: cut out the bad bits and you'll be left with true art. However, the problem is that this pruning operation does not leave very much at all, and that it is hard to see what is really happening anyway. Ironically, the art of the moment is taking the consequences of existing theory, but in a way that theory completely fails to comprehend. Just as minimal art can be seen as a follow-up – with other means – to Greenberg's theory, taking modernism to the utmost and beyond, one might regard today's art as the unexpected conclusion of the theory of coded choice. For instance, the realization that art is both a component of general visual culture and a prisoner in a semi-autonomous domain of its own, deters many artists from playing those domains off against each other, reflexively, but induces artists to manipulate them in conjunction, simultaneously – two different territories with two different publics. The realization that cultural identity has become a problem, that we have globalization and vague twilight zones, which form a patchwork of cultures, induces artists to nestle in those twilight zones as if they belonged there. I could go on for a while, but it all boils down to the same thing: certain problems are taken as a point of departure without reflection on those problems; what is more, it is almost suggested that a solution is possible in practice simply "by doing."

This smacks of poor and naive art, but there is a reason for that choice. To a large extent the problem is the reflexive discourse that has been theory's point of departure for years. For example, both media awareness and institutional awareness, as demanded by theory, pin down art on certain procedures, which can only be escaped by negating them. Imagine an art that is aware of the media it uses and of the role played by those media in society. An art aware of the fact that it can never escape from the institution of art, and aware of the problematic sides of a more socially engaged role without wanting to renounce that intention. Imagine that this art realizes all those things but does not want to get bogged down in reflection on the various positions for the simple reason that those positions *are* well known now, because reflection *has* taken place, in both art and theory. For this art it is a damn nuisance to enter into debate with that reflexive approach, simply because a next layer of consciousness is added as soon as you do. In other words, reflection on the reflexive position only sucks you further into the vortex of consciousness without coming up with any new solutions. Escape from this reflexive circle is only possible by pretending that the problem no longer exists, by acting as if a direct solution were possible, by exchanging the cynicism of the code for the optimism of the contact. A hazardous position, and one that can lead to a lot of trifling art. Nevertheless, art theory will have to reflect on its position: there is a kind of art which is escaping from its points of departure, and this requires theory to reflect upon itself.

Koen Brams

The Purloined Letter in an Adolescent's Bedroom as a Clip of Madonna in a Karaoke Café

"The purloined letter", "a clip of Madonna in a karaoke café" and "an adolescent's bedroom" – only three metaphors from a long list presented by Jeroen Boomgaard in his essay *New Communication, no Message*, a discourse on the place of theory in or with regard to today's art, and on the place of today's art in and with regard to society. Boomgaard's essay is certainly rife with metaphor, positively pulsating with it. For someone like myself who wants to convey a brief impression or summary of the text, the metaphors and rapid turns of phrase are equally rife with impediments and obstacles. Furthermore, polemic propositions alternate with ideas expressed in varying nuances, and the author often contradicts himself aloud.

What, then, is the central proposition of Boomgaard's text? Or, what are the propositions? By and large, he seems to be postulating two premises: 1) the art of today has scarcely any theoretical basis, nor does it need any, and 2) theory casts a nostalgic look back at its erstwhile position and by that token is incapable of coping with the art of today. I shall try to show that it is not a case of art and theory being engaged in mock battle, but that the author of the two aforementioned propositions has fallen victim to total confusion. Let me begin by asking the following question: what does Boomgaard mean by "the art of today"?

Living Art

Boomgaard makes constant reference to current art in his text. Sometimes he calls it "the art of this moment," sometimes "contemporary art" and sometimes "the art of today." What is contemporary art – or rather, who? Is it Karel Appel? Armando? Niek Kemps? Marlene Dumas? Aernout Mik? Or is it Job Koelewijn? Boomgaard does not commit himself, merely saying what contemporary art does, or saddling it with a negative definition. For example, he suggests that the art being produced today looks like the art of the sixties and seventies. Strictly speaking, this still doesn't tell us whether Boomgaard is referring to Appel and Armando, because they are still doing what they have always done. Only when we gain more insight into Boomgaard's perception of sixties and seventies art does it begin to dawn on us that he probably does not have Appel's and Armando's art in mind.

At first it seems funny to mention the names of Appel and Armando in a critique of a discourse on current art and contemporary theory. So Appel and Armando are not current or contemporary? Surely they are. Not just because they still have exhibitions in museums of modern art like the Stedelijk Museum in Amsterdam and the Stedelijk Museum voor Actuele Kunst in Ghent. In my opinion they are modern or contemporary because they influence the art being produced today and reflections on that art. They may well evoke a lot more, or other, negative reactions than they used to – among artists as well as critics and theorists – but that negative feedback also counts. If we go along with Boomgaard and focus exclusively on a particular kind of art – the art of today he claims is so similar to the art of the sixties and seventies – we do scant justice to the complexity of the situation of art, today. Boomgaard's reductive look at today's art swiftly leads to a comparison with the art of previous decades, the art of the sixties, seventies and eighties, and that art also gets a bad rap. But what is the art of the sixties, seventies or eighties? Or rather, who? Is it Karel Appel? Armando? Niek Kemps? Marlene Dumas? Again, the formulation seems too rhetorical to be true. But are we not justified in citing Appel and Armando when we talk about the art of the sixties and seventies? Of course we are. Any other presentation of the facts detracts from a conception of the complexity of the field of art, whether we are looking at 1974 or 1996.

To me the problem seems to be Boomgaard's use of the term "contemporary art" for something he assumes a number of people know what they are to understand by that. Boomgaard charges the term "contemporary art" with a number of connotations, expecting the initiated to know what he is talking about. I disagree with this. First, because his assumption of a "shared" understanding of what this contemporary art is supposed to be is doomed to founder on the limited comprehension of the speaker or listener. Second, because such an assumption or statement fails to take into account the complexity of the field of art, and that is the very thing that ought to be the ambition of all those who make statements about contemporary art or about art of the past. Any other stance is bound to lead to vague, partial, subjective, evasive statements about contemporary art and of course to the falsification of history with regard to art of the past.

Theory as a Leg

"In theoretical terms, art at the present time doesn't have a leg to stand on." This is the first sentence of Boomgaard's essay. What does he mean by it? Is there no theory for the art of the present time – whatever that might be? I seriously doubt it. Never before have we had so much theory, and I would find it odd if no theoretical framework existed for certain forms of art. Boomgaard's opening sentence suggests that the art of this moment does not itself provide some of its theoretical framework. If that is what he really thinks, I do not agree with him. Artists, all sorts of artists, not only make images but also produce a theoretical framework with those images. Often deliberately, in the form of propositions and manifesto's, sometimes unconsciously. Boomgaard's opening sentence contains a third proposition, an implicit reference to the past: art at the present time doesn't have a leg to stand on; things used to be different and better. I take strong exception to this historical reference. To me it is the most conclusive proof that we have only a partial understanding of art at the present time – as Boomgaard puts it. It is not *art* that lacks a theoretical leg to stand on, but the *viewer* of the art being currently produced. Surely Boomgaard cannot assume that a man like Duchamp, when he was experimenting with the ready-made, had a firmer theoretical leg to stand on than artists who are working today. If there *had* been a theoretical framework at the moment when Duchamp was experimenting with the ready-made, then it was his own theoretical framework. But what is there to prevent today's artists from doing the same thing?

The first sentence raises another problem, perhaps the most essential problem. Does art need theory for a leg to stand on? Is this a correct characterization of the relationship between art and theory? According to Boomgaard it is, for he continues: "But since contemporary art is once again fiddling at the boundaries of the notion of art, it is conceptual from the very start and needs theory as much as a fish needs water." I find this sentence, too, hard to take. Again, I disagree with the various implicit and explicit opinions it contains. Is contemporary art "fiddling" at the boundaries again, and the art of ten, twenty, thirty years ago to a lesser extent or not at all? Of course the vague term "contemporary art" puts paid to any discussion, it being unclear what Boomgaard means by it. But even with this terminological vagueness in the background, I would never wish to create the impression that contemporary art was fiddling at the boundaries and older art was not, or less. More fundamental, though, is my realization that Boomgaard's entire sentence is a tautology, and that he uses this tautology to cast an unfavorable light on today's art. Even if today's art is conceptual by its very nature, it does have an important theoretical component, doesn't it? What alternative is there? Boomgaard suggests something else: he argues that today's art, being conceptual anyway, needs theory as much as a fish needs water. This brings us to the crux of the discussion about the relationship between art and theory. Is theory something that is *per se* produced outside art? Boomgaard suggests that this is the case; I beg to differ. Is art something that is produced outside theory? Boomgaard says it is; I vehemently disagree. Can theory benefit from art? Boomgaard doesn't ask that question; my answer is affirmative.

Art and Theory, Part 1

To the question about the relationship between art and theory I have two answers, which are mutually relevant to a marked degree. The first is fundamental, the second pragmatic: the first is art-theoretical, the second sociological. The first has to do with the fundamentals of art and thus has a historical side as well. The second has to do with art as use, art as daily practice. Let us examine the first, fundamental answer. It is closely related to Boomgaard's proposition, which, however, he does not think through properly. I agree with Boomgaard when he writes that fiddling at the boundaries of the notion of art has a conceptual basis. Fiddling at the boundaries of the notion of art – and hence of the conceptual framework of art, or the theory of art – is in my opinion closely linked with the origins of art, its origin as a more or less autonomous system. As soon as art detaches itself from its exclusive patron, the religious apparatus, and also succeeds – at first in only a very small way – in detaching itself from the language it has spoken hitherto, the language of religion, it becomes both modern and autonomous. It develops its own art concept. Whereas previously it had only spoken its patron's language and operated solely under the umbrella of the religious system, henceforth it must rely on itself in the totally fragmented and fragmenting social field. From that moment, art's concerns are more than just its own. From that moment, art is more than simply self-referential. Its involvement in its own functioning, its self-referentiality, and its concomitant conceptualization are nevertheless fundamental to what we understand as art. The logical conclusion, then, must be that the conceptualization or the development of theory is intrinsic to our conception of art. Boomgaard is actually aware of the relationship between art's autonomy and its concomitant theorization, for together with Thierry de Duve he posits, "any reflection about art is preceded by the implicit statement that 'this is art'." The problem, though, is that he perceives a connection only between the "reflection on art" and the implicit pronouncement "this is art," whereas every artistic action has the implicit pronouncement "this is art" as its horizon. Another problem is that Boomgaard takes recourse solely to De Duve, who in turn takes Duchamp's ready-mades as his point of departure. In doing so, he conveys the impression that the autonomy of art is a twentieth-century problem. Boomgaard does not sufficiently think through Duchamp's ready-made, the twentieth-century articulation of the autonomy issue. He fails to go in search of the roots of art's autonomy, thereby repudiating art's essential connection with its theory.

Art and Theory, Part 2

Art's involvement with its theory is often denied or swept under the carpet. It is also often the butt of protest or aggression on the part of both artists and critics, or the public in general. Art has absolutely nothing to do with conceptualization, they say; art is the product of a flash of brilliance, the outcome of waiting patiently and making the right move at the right moment. But there is no such thing as the unmediated act, not with Appel, not even with Pollock. Every form of mediation or discourse is tantamount to a reflection of what it means to engage in artistic activity and not in other autonomous disciplines such as football, politics or biology.

Football, politics and biology bring us almost automatically to the second argument for speaking about a close relationship between art and theory or theorization. In a certain sense the second argument compels me to modify the first one slightly. Instead of talking about the absolute differences between art, football, politics or biology, perhaps it makes more sense to talk about relative differences. Art is autonomous, but not in an absolute sense. The boundaries of art are constantly put to the test, by artists, critics and also by "others" – that is what fiddling at the boundaries of the notion of art means. The proposition just formulated has been slightly modified and now posits that the autonomous moment of art inevitably has an autoreflexive and conceptual component. It is precisely for the sake of that relative autonomy, which Boomgaard *does* acknowledge, defining it in his own inimitable way as art "confined in its own small cage but part of a permanent and unavoidable flow," that it is altogether wrong to speak of contemporary art in such terms as "it's all been seen before." If there already are so many similarities, even downright duplicates or "resurrections," the work of art still means something different. So why speak of the return of sixties and seventies art? Why bring up *déjà vu* if *déjà su* is excluded in the first place? It is not possible to pass the same judgment on a work that is the same as, or resembles, a work made ten, twenty, thirty years earlier. Why does Boomgaard concur with the idea of the autonomy of art, and also with the idea of the relative autonomy of art, only to reject it in the case of the art of today?

Focusing on art's relative autonomy now, we are chiefly interested in the way art functions in the world. I ought immediately to add: and how art theory functions in the world. Is making art or being otherwise involved in art conceivable at all without discursive mediation? I don't think so. When we want to talk about images, we seldom resort to images exclusively. What we resort to – perhaps from laziness or for the sake of convenience, I won't say which – are words. Often little more than chatter, voices, but sometimes theoretical constructions as well. It doesn't matter as far as my proposition is concerned. The lightest theoretical preoccupation – the theoretical preoccupation that does make a difference, a difference in meaning – suffices to endorse my proposition. Even chatter (the usual art reviews, interviews with artists, conversations at openings) can mask small theoretical preoccupations. Not inspired thoughts perhaps, maybe unpleasant, but they are there, and they are not hard to trace. There's no such thing as art without thoughts. There's no such thing as art without conceptualization or theorization – however modest or unpleasant. Art like that simply does not exist.

Boomgaard makes a particular point of playing off contemporary art against theory and vice versa. Anyone capable of abstraction can indeed conceive of a dividing line between something like art on the one side and theory on the other. However, as I have been trying to say, there is an essential theoretical moment when we are talking about art, and art without discursive mediation is simply out of the question. But even if we turn it into an abstraction for a minute and arrive at the two abstract categories "art" and "theory," does it make any sense to juxtapose the two, as Boomgaard does? Instead of a static view that places art and theory opposite each other like two blocks, I adopt a dynamic view. Art and theory behave towards each other dynamically. Art snaffles entire theories or bits and pieces of theories, theory is the parasite of art, or art is for theory the field in which ideas can be tested. If art and theory are at each other's throats, it is due to the fact that art and theory often benefit from each other unconsciously without thematizing that intensive exchange. When attention is paid to the exchange, as in Boomgaard's text, it is often understood as one-way traffic: art in search of a theoretical leg to stand on, and theory as a solipsistic discipline, a discipline that is self-sufficient. My proposition is that art and theory are related, and that this relationship often remains hidden, either because the artist or theorist keep it hidden from view (so that art or theory retain the virginal aura of the autonomous act of creation), or because the artist or theorist are unaware of it. With a view to initiating a deliberate and fruitful exchange, the Jan van Eyck Academy has two separate departments for art and theory. Art does not have a little sub-department for theory, and the same applies vice versa. The two disciplines formulate their own points of departure but can join forces to conduct research and mount projects. Art is not theory's handmaid, nor is theory art's slave; they interact.

In this World

But according to Boomgaard it is today's art that lacks a theoretical leg to stand on. Let us take a final look at his text. Hitherto I have dwelt only on the first two sentences, albeit two whopping sentences. What else can we learn from his text?

One of the problems is the constant confusion between the intentions which Boomgaard imputes to art, his criticism of those intentions, his perception of the works of art that result from them, other people's criticism of those works, the intentions Boomgaard imputes to the critics, and so forth. In one way or another it all comes back to the intention of art or of theory. Instead of calling a spade a spade, he tends to cite large and hence elusive categories like "art and theory," "the art of the sixties, seventies, eighties and the art of today." An example: "... history was already disposed of in theory as an outmoded concept. And it is partly the consequences of this that the younger generation are dragging along with them." And he continues: "You can hardly call history an arbitrary construction and at the same time use the reproach of a lack of historical awareness." Has anyone ever had such a black-and-white view of "history" and about the subjective element in recorded history? And if so, are artists aware of this? If they are, as Boomgaard suggests, there is no better proof for my proposition that artists have a thoroughly discursive *and* theoretical cast of mind.

I should like to describe Boomgaard's argument as an example of deliberate insincerity, intellectual laziness or misplaced cantankerousness. Let me illustrate this by citing the ideas Boomgaard advances about the second theme of his text, i.e. the issue of art's place in or in terms of the social field. That issue refers to the question of art and engagement. The hypothesis that constantly recurs in Boomgaard's text, although not for a single moment itself the subject of a critical thematization, is the assumption that art cannot be simultaneously autonomous (relatively speaking) and engaged. There are of course countless examples of works of art, which show a total lack of reflection on the relation between the autonomous moment of art and its possible involvement in the social field. It does, however, seem that Boomgaard is cognizant only of that kind of art. He keeps on referring to the naivety of art. There is some justification for this, I grant you, but can't he cite any examples of works of art which are the result of an intellectual approach to the relative autonomy of art, and to art's involvement in the social field in which it will function? We do not get to read these examples, which range from, say, Marcel Broodthaers via Daniel Buren to Maria Eichhorn. What we *are* given to read are repeated, vague insinuations.

Why doesn't he give us some examples of the inspiring endeavors to participate, by way of the reflected autonomy of art, in a production which has broad social significance? Why does Boomgaard give us such a black-and-white impression of the autonomous moment of art compared with art's ambition to be involved in the social field? Art's relative autonomy is not in itself an impediment to participation in the social production of meaning? Or is the refusal to grant art that role on a par with the denial of the discursive element in art? Is autonomy the same as the total absence of any form of discourse? Is Jeroen Boomgaard frightened of the meaning of the work of art? If so, he is not the only one, alas.

Jeroen Boomgaard and Koen Brams

Debate

Valentijn Byvanck

Jeroen Boomgaard, did Koen Brams give a fair rendering of your points of view?

Jeroen Boomgaard

I think my presentation today already solved many misunderstandings because I said things differently from what Brams gathered from my article. Of course art and theory interact. It's only natural. Of course art always has a theoretical component – these are points which I myself made. The fact that I wrote in my article in *A-Prior* that art doesn't have a leg to stand on at the present time, is a figure of speech, rhetoric. Surely an editor ought to know that. An editor who gets bogged down in the first two sentences of an article is not very confidence inspiring anyway. It is a fact that the autonomy of art begins many decades earlier, but if you had to explain that in every article, *De Witte Raaf* would be thicker and even more unreadable than it is already in danger of becoming.

If you're discussing today's art and need to include Appel and Armando, I doubt whether that article would ever get written. Nor do I think that all these different issues have a place in a theoretical programme at the Jan van Eyck Academy. Of course you simplify things when you develop a theory or take up a theoretical position. You're talking about certain things and you characterize them, for instance as art of this moment which seems to be turning away from theory, art which does not want to make theoretical statements. This is obviously itself a theory, or implies one. Brams interpreted my remark that theoretically art does not have a leg to stand on as meaning that art is searching for a theory. Well, that's his interpretation, but it is totally incorrect. Perhaps he wishes it weren't, for his department, but it is absolutely not the case. All I meant was that from a theoretical point of view, art is a-theoretical. Again: rhetoric, and usually recognized as such by a good reader. And then there was that sentence about art needing theory as much as a fish needs water. Yes, it was a somewhat implicit reference to a statement made by Barnett Newman – in a little Witte de With book – who said that art needs theory the way a bird needs ornithology, and I varied that statement slightly. Of course the two always have something to do with each other. Art always swims in theory, just as theory keeps afloat with the aid of art. Whether they like it or not, they can't do without each other.

What I thought was interesting – and Brams ignores this – is that all kinds of theoretical debates in what are usually unimpeachable critical journals – not *Kunstbeeld* or anything of that kind, but *De Witte Raaf* – have recently been grumbling about the art of this moment. And by the art of this moment I don't mean Armando and Appel, who had their theoretical impulse years and years ago, but artists who, while still quite young, took up a stance implicitly or explicitly against certain kinds of art. And in those debates you could hear what sounded like old men grumbling that it had all been seen before. So that is not my point either: that it has all been seen before. It is one of the accusations which are made, and the rhetoric of my article in *A-Prior* is that I start by citing those accusations so that the reader will think, "my goodness, isn't he negative about modern art?" Only later do I show that the accusations contain certain postulates, which are perhaps not entirely justifiable. It's one way of building up an article, but it needs a smart reader. You don't always get one.

Koen Brams

The use of figures of speech is one of the problems about how Boomgaard builds up arguments: one simply doesn't know where he stands and what it's all about. And let me come back to your first point: you yourself said with regard to the first sentence of your own article that you were playing devil's advocate, and you're already completely off course, because it's not about art versus theory or theory versus art. You allege that artists have a certain way of dealing with the autonomous moment of art and the institutional moment of art as opposed to an art that formulates its own problems on the basis of that autonomous moment. You were just saying that there was and perhaps still is art, which examines its own institutional position. And so my proposition is that every artist can be perfectly aware of that discussion but then, proceeding from that basis, formulates his own problems, and in that sense certainly does have, or can create, a theoretical leg to stand on. And despite what you claim, critical theory can cope with that very well indeed.

Audience

I'd like to hear from the speakers what the difference is between an artist's theory and a theorist's theory. Does an artist really need a theory, a kind of personal logic? At present they seem to overlap.

Koen Brams

That's one of Boomgaard's problems really, although he disagrees. But when he talks about art he doesn't need any theory, and when he talks about theory he suddenly comes up with Greenberg. And so, again: he makes a comparison between the two blocks.

Audience

Does theory only exist from the moment it is extracted from the work?

Jeroen Boomgaard

It has already been extracted. Of course there is a theoretical side and a production side: free expression is a theory if you believe it comes from inside. It's all right to believe that it comes from inside, but that is a theoretical conception and it determines what comes from inside. The theory has already been formulated, but it is only one theory; on the production side you don't usually have one consistent theory. Thank goodness, otherwise you'd get illustrations to a story. But there are theoretical components. On the other hand, the theorist tries to formulate a stance which connects things, makes them into a story. That is limiting, it's smaller of course, or larger; theory and art keep dancing around each other and that's what makes it interesting. They confirm and negate each other all the time. And what is so interesting in our times, I think, is that it's happening again at this moment, in the very art about which – although Brams denies it – older theorists are complaining, in *De Witte Raaf* too. Theory is under discussion in a way that presents a huge challenge.

Koen Brams

You realize that all art and every work of art is mediated discursively, but you try to negate that as much as possible when you're dealing with art. That's your problem.

Jeroen Boomgaard

No. My point of departure is that today's art appears to operate from a modernistic stance but is actually implementing postmodern axioms, taking them beyond theory by putting them into practice. Artists are often admonished for not adopting a stance, but postmodernism has said: choosing a stance is irrelevant. It's and-and. It's only now that the and-and concept is being used in art.

Koen Brams

It is totally unclear what position you are adopting, where you stand and what period you are addressing. I refuse to talk to you any more about the sixties or whatever. You've got to be serious. I can't understand how an art historian can behave like this.

Jeroen Boomgaard

How is an art historian supposed to behave?

Koen Brams

Make a statement. A statement about the sixties, as you did in your talk here. It's quite enlightening really, and you can be pinned down somewhere. When you write, you usually say something and then turn it around. That makes it quite obvious that you don't want to make a statement and eliminate yourself as a participant in the discussion.

Jeroen Boomgaard

No. I offer an opportunity, an opening, to think about theory and to see what new avenues are open to it. It's not clear to me yet.

Valentijn Byvanck

Koen Brams, you seem to condemn Boomgaard's strategy of shifting positions as dishonest. But to me it seems that this strategy provides room for the reader to select his own point of view on the basis of his own experience and knowledge of art. I don't see the moral fault of it, nor am I convinced that this suggestion of anchoring theory in personal integrity would benefit theory *an sich*.

Jeroen Boomgaard

Here we have a fundamental problem with regard to that theoretical position. Myself, I detest texts which explicitly state their position and adopt a viewpoint. I lose all interest in them. I am trying to open up a position for the reader, not to close one. And of course that is a trick, you might even say a didactic trick. That is why I start by showing my reader a negative viewpoint which I then turn around to show that is has two sides. What is happening really – that is the final question – and how are we to cope with it? And then you can say: the answer has been there for a long time and yes, you can write it too. The result is a different kind of article. But that's not what interests me most. Lots of authors have quite evident stances and can go on describing their position till the cows come home, but I usually give up after the first two sentences.

Valentijn Byvanck

Koen Brams, how is one a better theorist by not chopping and changing all the time?

Koen Brams

I'm not saying it's wrong, it's the way Boomgaard does it that's wrong.

Audience

So tell us what's right and what isn't.

Koen Brams

I can only tell you what I am looking for. There are a lot of ways of getting there. That's why I'm saying that when someone explains his position and tells us what he has seen and experienced and erects theoretical constructions around it or applies a particular theory to it, I can find that very interesting. Simply, where do I want to go? I want a text to teach me something. That is what theory does.

Valentijn Byvanck

Aren't you really saying that there is good and bad theory, convincing and non-convincing theory?

Koen Brams

Boomgaard does not present a theory, but presents a number of theoretical points of departure. So when he says a work of art is related to visual culture he is asking us to think about that work and visual culture. That is not a theoretical statement, but at best a basis for one.

Jeroen Boomgaard

I'm curious about that theory of yours which combines Karel Appel and Armando.

Koen Brams

I never said that a theory could be conceived for that.

Jeroen Boomgaard

But how can you consider all those different positions in one article? How on earth is it possible?

Koen Brams

I said that when you use the term "contemporary art" in an article there's simply no way of getting a grasp on it. The reason I think of Karel Appel is that there's a lot to be said about the feedback from his art, and the theory that comes with it, for what is going on in art today. What I am saying is that you have a very limited, very reductive view of what is going on in art today. That's what I meant by citing Karel Appel and Armando. And I think it's a pity, that's all.

Jeroen Boomgaard

Then you evidently skipped half the article. Further on I say what contemporary art is. Artists are taking to the streets again, they seek direct interaction with the public, and focus on the small gesture, the autobiographical aspect. It doesn't look like Karel Appel or Armando, as I explain later on in the article. When you say contemporary art, you mean a certain kind of production that advertises itself in galleries and exhibitions and says: this is new art. It's not all that complicated. It is a simplification, but a necessary one. Who can write an article on the production of Orgacom and artists like that who exhibit an odd kind of naivety, and at the same time write about Armando, Dumas and Appel?

Audience

On the subject of differences between art and theory: an artist can combine different things in a work without any problem at all. The problem is the theory that has to seek the connections and explain.

Audience

What is a theoretical statement about a work of art? Is everything a critic writes theory?

Jeroen Boomgaard

Well, I don't think it's an easy position. Today's art critics, on average, simply describe a work, telling us whether it's enjoyable or not. The moment you want to make an analysis of the work, you must have a theory from which to approach it. And one of the points I make in my article is that I don't think there is a terribly clear theory at all, and that makes it more exciting. You're skating on slippery ice here, because a lot of theoretical positions are broached, but they are not thought through and falsified. This produces an ambiguity that makes you think: what has this to do with me? Is it superficial eyewash or does it mean something? And that is an interesting point.

Koen Brams

Imagine art criticism without the theories or budding theories or fragments which artists present in interviews, when they invite critics and other artists to their studios, when they produce their own books. Imagine that's all you have to go by, as an art critic or a theorist. What can you do in such a situation? I find that role most exciting.

Audience

Does that mean you want the work of art to be your only informant?

Koen Brams

No, that's not what I mean. It's an impossible position. But if you ask me what position interests me as a critic, the answer would be somewhere utopian. Trying to say something that interests me, discovering meanings. We're talking here about what position I think is interesting. Of course it's a utopian situation. If I draw attention to an aspect of a work of art by thinking about it, something that contributes to a discussion about that work, then I have achieved something. I think that's an interesting position, but such ideas are very scarce. I once, with a team of *De Witte Raaf*, assembled an encyclopedia of clichés, by sifting through everything that had ever been said and written about art and artworks. It was one of my most instructive experiences: to see how meagre, how arid the development of ideas is. That was the negative side, but it was incredibly amusing and instructive, because I also kept bumping into myself.

Jeroen Boomgaard

That's exactly what it's about: to open up the situation, not close it. It can be done in different way from Derrida's: by building up an argument that addresses art from different positions and leaves it to the reader to consider those different positions.

Audience

Artists are accused of not knowing enough about the sixties. What can be done about it? There's an awful lot of artist hype, so how can they learn about it?

Jeroen Boomgaard

As an art historian I take it to heart that artists do not (want to) know about it, but it is of course a dangerous point to keep harping on. We have a problem with the art of the sixties: it had an ideal that somehow got lost, damaged, however you choose to describe it. Knowledge of that ideal is also knowledge of its failure. Naivety can sometimes be a strategy. Artists appeal to all kinds of things, to their innermost feelings, to sincerity, but does that matter so much to me when I look at their work? A work is not sincere when I look at it. Sincerity – to me it is a modernistic term and a moral category that has absolutely nothing to do with art. I don't give a damn about sincerity in a work of art. Perhaps the artist fools me – I hope so. I think that might be very interesting.

I feel no need to refer to the sixties in my classes. The effect would be stifling. If work reverts to the sixties, one should examine how it works at this moment, and what happens with it now. One should not say: it's a repetition. Stifling the present by referring to the past has happened frequently. That was my stance with regard to history: history has been abolished in postmodernism. Koen Brams thinks that a great number of artists don't know this, but it has become such a widespread concept, not only in theory but in practice too: amusement-park practice, we're living it. We're living history as pure construction, something that can be re-invented every day. The consequence is that the sixties are something you can refer to or not, know or not know, and apparently it does not matter to artists. We can adopt a moralizing attitude, but it is not the most interesting position. Bram's and my proposition – and here we are in complete agreement – is that theory is both preceding art and limping along behind it, and trying to cobble something together which can't be cobbled together. All those artists' propositions are implicitly theoretical; they are theoretical statements.

III. The Curator

Iwona Blazwick

Catherine David

Foreword

Over the past two decades, curators of contemporary art have become high profile professionals. They juggle a number of tasks that tend to multiply with the rising status of the profession. They are production assistants, exhibition organizers, art scouts, taste guides and intellectuals of sorts to a varied (and sometimes fastidious) art audience. The divergent functions put high pressure on the curator's shoulders. Much of this is the result of the exalted art market which demands that curators produce shows at a high pace across the globe. It catapults some curators into a stardom much greater than that of the artists whose work they exhibit, and the institutions they represent.

Witte de With organized this evening in light of these developments. What should be expected of the curator? What are the curator's responsibilities, tasks, and limits within the constantly changing field of contemporary art? Iwona Blazwick, director of Whitechapel Art Gallery, addresses these questions from her experience of setting up the new presentations in the Tate Modern. Catherine David, who organized *Documenta X* and is currently director of Witte de With, contends that the curator, more than a promoter, should focus more and more on esthetic practices that take place outside the established art circuit.

The debate, entitled *The New Curator*, was held on May 31, 2001.

Iwona Blazwick

Brushing against the Grain of History

As soon as works of art enter a collection they become one episode in a larger narrative, organized and displayed in particular sequences, with a cast of characters and developments. This narrative comes eventually to represent a history. In the case of the modern museum, such as the Museum of Modern Art in New York the Centre Pompidou in Paris or the Tate Gallery in London, that history has become *the* story of modern art. And as the artist Daniel Buren has commented, it is a history transformed by the institution into nature.

In fact this seems to have been borne out by the reaction of some critics to the new display of the collection at Tate Modern. Some complain that the works have been, well, curated – as if for the first time. As if, in fact, prior to this reconfiguration, works of art had arrived on the walls by some process of natural selection, in a preordained order.

The notion of creating master narratives has of course been thoroughly investigated by artists, critics and historians for some time; the canon of art history and the museum's relation to it has been debated in a wider theoretical context informed by semiology, Marxism, feminism, psychoanalysis, analytical philosophy and the politics of identity. Most modern collections which have asserted esthetic values and historical accounts as objective, autonomous and universal have been reappraised as subjective, contingent and western in their perspective.

The advent of Tate Modern, a new museum opening at the beginning of the twenty-first century, has provided a unique opportunity to examine the conventions and assumptions around the display of a collection, not only in terms of its organizing principles, but also in consideration of the exhibition itself as a form of discourse.

The organizing principle which has come to dominate most modernist collections around the world was inspired by Alfred H. Barr's flow chart. Devised in 1936 to accompany the exhibition *Cubism and Abstract Art* it does more than simply trace a chronology; Barr created a didactic diagram which charted a stylistic evolution of "isms", a succession of European avant-garde movements which suggested progress towards abstraction as point zero. In its neo-scientific style and its authoritative clarity it provided a paradigm for the understanding and display of modern and contemporary art which has dominated museum practice. Barr's assumption was that modern art developed in a series of self-determining advances towards a concentration of esthetic experiences vested in form rather than content, isolated from the contingencies of the world. It is a system of categorization which is still used to delineate art into periods and movements suggesting that individual practice can be encompassed in broad tendencies, which neatly begin and end, each in reaction to the last. This form of linear evolution cannot however account so neatly for individuals – for example where would one situate Francis Bacon? Nor does it reflect synchronicity – the fact that Picasso and Warhol were alive and active at the same time. Most art originating from beyond the NATO alliance countries, or art which adheres to pre-modernist traditions or radically challenges the modernist line, is also excluded. As the art historian Linda Nochlin has commented, we should not mistake chronology for history.

Another reason for us to explore alternatives to the linear chronology were informed by the actual architecture of Bankside. The galleries dedicated to the collection at Bankside are arranged on two floors and organized into four architecturally coherent suites. The Tate has an incredible architectural vocabulary of spaces, ranging from the autonomous purity of the white cube, to rooms which suddenly admit exhilarating views across London. The complexity of the floor plan and the sheer size of each suite, demanded a new approach. There was a strong possibility that visitors might choose to visit only one of the four suites. The view, advocated by many voices throughout the consultation process was that each suite should offer some kind of rounded experience of the twentieth century where the historic would be encountered in dialogue with the contemporary. This suggested that we either adopt four parallel yet distinct chronologies, or adopt four themes which were sufficiently flexible and provocative to contain displays from throughout the century.

Through a process of brainstorming and debate, key questions emerged. Working closely with the curator Frances Morris and with input from our education curator, Caro Howell, we came up with a number of alternative models, experiments, some of which I thought I would share with you.

The first focused on art and society. We asked whether it was possible to reconnect art with social and cultural history, grouping works of art according to the prevailing themes of the twentieth century. The advantages were that art would be reconnected with the conditions of its production. The disadvantages that it could be misinterpreted as merely a symptom of its time. And how could we represent history on a global scale particularly within the confines of the collection in its primarily European and North American focus.

The second pertained to defining moments. Art meets the world through the medium of the exhibition, the publication, the manifesto: we explored the idea of plotting a chronology within the framework of an exhibition history. This model unites art, installation and ideas, showing how contemporaries emerged and peer groups were formed, and how institutions play a part in shaping histories. But how could we restage exhibitions – and would this be meaningful to a broad, uninitiated public?

The third dealt with geographies. This was inspired by the Centre Pompidou's *Paris/Moscow*, or *Paris/New York* shows, we looked at art in relation to cities as international centers. There is a powerful relationship between modernism, modernity and the metropolis. Yet this arrangement not only highlighted the gaps in the collection, but was also likely to reinforce a hierarchy of the west and the rest.

Finally, we explored various strategies of making. We invited a number of artists, curators, educators and academics to join in the brainstorming and to respond to some of our ideas. Without exception the invited artists plumped for this approach. The idea of concentrating on process puts the viewer in a very tangible relation with the work of art, reiterating Lawrence Weiner's dictum, "Learn to read Art." However we had of course to recognize that many artists can be categorized under all of these methodologies – and on a purely formal level it was clear that whole sections could look pretty homogeneous.

These are just some of the many options we explored. And in a sense all of them have in some way been folded into our final solution. Ultimately we decided to focus on subject matter. We speculated as to whether form and content might fall into any particular categories and found ourselves considering a form of classification, which is almost as old as the making of art itself, the genre. Although formally defined as genres in the seventeenth century, certain types of subject matter have prevailed throughout western art. Broadly speaking, for the purposes of this process, we have defined these as the still life, the landscape, the human figure, including portraiture and the nude, and the historic narrative or allegory. We considered whether these typologies could have any relevance today. Certainly the supposed boundaries of conventional genres and their embeddedness in hierarchical social and political structures have inspired artists to acts of vanguardist transgression and departure. Yet even taking account of this trajectory towards the autonomous work of art that underlines the modernist sensibility, it appeared that these subjects or forms still adhered. If however, another overwhelming tendency within modern and contemporary art can be seen as a move from illustration and metaphor to a material and subjective reality, so these categories themselves can be seen in terms of an expanded field. This is not to suggest an evolution, but a radical expansion in time and space. For landscape therefore, one might read environment; for the nude, the body; for still life, real life; and for history, society.

Of course these broad themes overlap. It is also clear that many artistic practices are relevant to more than one. They are not being imposed however, as static, rigidly defining categories. Some artists may, over time, be shown in all four suites, reflecting both the broad resonance of their practice and the contingency of interpretation. The open-endedness of these thematic constructions in fact allows for an anthology of exhibition types, from the solo show, a single work in focus, the analysis of one movement or medium, to the use of a theme to bring together artists from across the century.

I wanted to look in a little more detail at each theme and to pick out certain displays devised by Tate curators.

Landscape/Matter/Environment

The genre of landscape is primarily understood as a representation of a rural or urban scene, which might be topographic, metaphoric or sublime. But it might also encompass the creation of phenomenal environments of space, light, texture and color. A map is a form of landscape, a diagrammatic system for containment, ownership and territorial aggression. Mapping through walking brings out a performative approach. Artists have brought the actual substance of nature into the gallery, or have gone out to make work in and from the landscape, documenting their actions through photographs and texts. Scientific discoveries about the underlying patterns and structures in organisms have inspired new artistic languages. An exploration of growth and form as a means towards abstraction might feature here, as well as the notion of archaeology and geology, wherein the landscape becomes a historic sedimentation, an analogue for time. This genre reconceived at Tate Modern as Landscape/Matter/Environment, also includes the zone of the imaginary, uncanny dreamscapes, symbolic visualizations of anxiety and desire.

Still Life/Object/Real Life

Still life was traditionally regarded as the most humble and conservative of genres. Over the last hundred years, however, it has become the focus of many of the most radical innovations in art. It is the ubiquity, and on one level, the timelessness of foodstuffs and vessels that make them both immediate and economical for artists to work with, and at the same time capable of evoking a universal chord of recognition. Still Life/Object/ Real Life shows the still life as a springboard for the sculptural analysis of ideal forms, or for optical adventures in the effect of color. In their deployment of the latest methods of production, design and style, the works here might provide a picture of an era. For some artists, they represent a celebration of the everyday, or a rejection, through the use of the ready made of esthetic value, or a critique of consumer capitalism. Their forms can be both erotic and melancholy, as much signifiers of desire as intimations of mortality. As symbols of the process of labor, the utilitarian objects of the still life have also been deployed as the tools of revolution.

Nude/Action/Body

A preoccupation with the human figure has and will remain a constant through art. In the modern period however it has been increasingly animated, ritualized and deconstructed, as artists have made the body both subject and object.

Within an overall framework titled Nude/Action/Body, the conventions of the nude as a means of exploring anatomy, movement and formal composition within the hermetic space of the studio is juxtaposed with a range of works that rupture and fragment idealized beauty. Here we encounter the body as a symbol for states of being, from alienation to abjection, from *jouissance* to mortality. The female body is reclaimed from the objectification of the male gaze to the assertion of an active, subjective female identity. In the movement of art from representation to reality, artists use their own bodies, staging and recording actions that test physical endurance or confront social taboos. The body in question might be an absent presence, signified only by traces; it might be that of the viewer. As audience we might find ourselves performing a work, participate in its meaning by virtue of our own actions and field of perception.

History/Memory/Society

The history painting, as contested a genre as the nude, is perhaps more difficult to define from a contemporary standpoint. Its conventions can, however, be seen as a fundamental dynamic behind two prevailing tendencies in modern and contemporary art – autonomy and engagement. The "painting of modern life" to use Baudelaire's term, might be understood as picturing history. History/Memory/Society draws together works which picture both the epic and the everyday, from the great convulsions of our times encompassed by wars, exile and the ruthless pursuit of ideology, to the celebration of systems of belief and the power of cultural icons. The rise of the media and mass communication might be seen as an undercurrent informing and shaping these representations. At the same time, this framework embraces both realist and abstract artists who have sought to change history itself, by erasing what had gone before and creating a new present. Their utopian strategies included breaking down boundaries between form and function, thus offering a synthesis of fine art, product design, architecture and graphics, the latter a potent medium in the circulation of ideas through the form of the manifesto. The call for revolution resonates here and might be encountered as protest or play.

The challenge for the museum of art today is twofold. Can we create the museum envisaged by artists, critics and the range of communities that constitute our public, one that can, in the words of Andreas Huysen, work with changes, refine its strategies of representation and offer its spaces as sites of cultural contestation? Can we also create conditions of viewing which reflect artistic intention, celebrate the esthetic and intellectual achievement of those artists whose works are part of our national patrimony and provide lucid and informative critical frameworks for their enjoyment and understanding? Over a five year period we will see not one, but many stories of the twentieth and twenty-first centuries, understood through a shifting and multifaceted perspective. They will allow flexibility, dynamism and a continued commitment to new scholarship and new ways of seeing and of understanding the past in relation to the present.

Catherine David

The New Curator

There are two realities about contemporary curatorship. One is the instrumentalization and spectacularization of art, a "contemporary art" which, in the last fifteen years has become a specialized category of cultural consumerism. This development is not only the result of the market. Institutions, too, have been acting in questionable ways. The curatorial attitudes described in Valentijn Byvanck's introduction are the products of the current exhibition industry, in which the curator is really more of a promoter. I believe that as a curator you can make a choice as to whether you wish to be a promoter or opt for a more critical approach.

The second reality of contemporary art has to do with the development of contemporary practices into fields of exploration that are not necessarily related to art history. Starting in the 1950s, often associated with 1970s art practices, and increasingly visible in the articulation of artistic practices today, artists refer more and more to the anthropological, social, and political dimensions of culture. Most of the challenging works of the last fifteen years attempt to represent the complexity of contemporary societies. Unlike the promoter, the curator must deal with this new situation and work with the realization that an exhibition in an institution is no longer the alpha and omega of the artist's presentation. The curator must also work outside the institution and find ways to circulate projects in alternative social and cultural spaces. I could list many proposals that do so. For instance Fareed Armaly's *From/To* at Witte de With (1999), which introduced very complex politically charged cultural phenomena in a network involving both the three-dimensional real and temporary space of the exhibition and the two-dimensional space of the Internet. *From/To* presented a highly conflicting body of works with virtual and real dimensions, providing a representation of possible Palestinian cultures in Palestine and the Diaspora. Another example is the brilliant exhibition organized by Hilton Judin and more than twenty other people in the Netherlands Architecture Institute titled *Blank*.

1. *Blank. Apartheid, Architecture, and After*, Netherlands Architecture Institute, Rotterdam, December 17, 1998 – April 4, 1999.

Apartheid, Architecture, and After.[1] This was a very original, radical proposal to posit an anthropological landscape in between cultural space, architectural heritage and the politics of apartheid. A third example is the wonderful presentation of Italian design from the sixties and seventies by Andrea Branzi in the Triennial in Milan, which featured a huge platform with a flow of objects punctuated by monitors projecting important films from those years by Rossellini and Pasolini. In a disturbing project for the same Triennial in Milan, Daniele del Giudici assembled a *Uomo Italianicus* at the turn of the twentieth century, creating an identity with objects ranging from the jail summons from the *Mani Pulite* period, to Pasolini's wonderful manuscript in which he mentions for the first time "Dopo Historia," post-history, to very surprising computer-images and photographs from many Arabic sites.

These models for curating today pose an alternative to mere promotion, or the meaningless juxtaposition of works. They were not necessarily appreciated by the press, certainly not the artistic press, which prefers to focus on big bombastic exhibitions, but they nevertheless contributed to the circulation of ideas and images, and suggested a redefinition of the position of the curator in contemporary society.

None of this is really new. As far back as the early avant-garde movements in the twenties and thirties – think of Duchamp or Malevich – the curator acted as a catalyst, as someone able to articulate, render dynamic and visible, things or processes not immediately perceived by the audience, and sometimes not even by the artists and producers themselves. The curator has always dealt with experimental practices, finding new conditions for the production and the diffusion of works into contemporary society. Esthetic practices spring from processes of experiment, discussion and debate. We have to be very visionary and active to preserve and develop those processes. Without them, esthetic practices are often reduced to a pure collection of objects produced without meaning and unrelated to contemporary culture and society; they signify the esthetization of problems rather than a critical questioning.

At this experimental moment, we must also connect to various audiences. I never use the word "big" audiences because I think the idea is very tiring. Current audiences do not constitute a single homogeneous body, but instead a collection of original and sometimes very conflicting knowledges and memories. In future years, especially in megalopolic circumstances, the make-up of the complex post-colonial population can only become more heterogeneous. It is not the task of curators to seduce these audiences. Instead, they should interfere, discuss and be in touch with these heterogeneous groups, including of course those people who have little affinity with the classical place of the museum or art institution. Curators will have to work more and more on translations, on transitions, on transmediations. Some might view this as a utopian idea. But if you are a little more modest and live consciously as a member of your society, if you try to understand and interact, you may not find many spectacular things, but you do discover many possible ways of communicating with these modern and diverse audiences.

Iwona Blazwick described the role of the curator in a big museum as attempting to articulate modern, modernist, and contemporary collections. I am more interested in curatorial practices that mediate between heterogeneous audiences, and the contemporary production of esthetic values and diverse, sometimes antagonistic cultural practices, disciplines and areas of competence. In light of this, I prefer the phrase "staging events," to "making exhibitions." With the term "exhibition" you prepare people for a very static, framed experience. It signals a classical situation in which there is a unity of time, space and action. But contemporary proposals from artists with diverse geographical and cultural backgrounds do not necessarily explore only one space and time, and they do not necessarily reflect a unified narrative, so you have to articulate different places, and different temporalities.

Of course people will never understand if you are not changing the rules of the game. You must communicate carefully what you're doing and what it is about, and make clear that something happens at a certain moment. This sounds like a mere technical problem, yet if you don't take it seriously, it can end in a nightmare, and the castration of the work. It happened to me, as I am sure it happened to you, that I entered a certain space to view a project and could not figure out whether I was too early or too late. This failure to communicate a project results not only in logistical problems, but also in a senseless esthetization of objects. It is therefore of paramount importance for a curator to accompany the work, mediate the production to keep the phenomenon alive and productive, and avoid mere esthetization.

Another strategy I would like to stress, evoked by Iwona Blazwick in her discussion of the Tate Modern's strategies of presenting its collections, focuses on possible ways of showing the collection in a polemical and open way. I agree with Blazwick that the exhibition *Les magiciens de la terre* was crucial, because of the event it was and because of the huge critical attention it received. But I think the exhibition itself was wrongheaded. Instead of making people aware of the complex temporalities of phenomena which occurred differently in different places, the exhibition was reproducing the cliché of the modernist invention versus the peripheral replica or adaptation. It reflected the romantic desire for egotism and expressed a neo-colonial view on contemporary esthetical production in the non-western world. For Brazil, instead of showing an important modern avant-garde artist like Helio Oiticica, it showed works from Macumba. In Brazil, you would never see a real Macumba if you were not initiated in this tradition, and certainly not in a museum. Second, Brazilians consider it a non-modernistic object and tool, and will never introduce it in an art exhibition. For Mexico, the presentation was even worse. Instead of showing for instance one of the muralists, the exhibition introduced a work in papier-mâché that would never have been shown in a museum of modern art in Mexico City. The exhibition showed, in short, what many people are still expecting from these countries: feathers, colors, earth, very traditional materials. In light of this, it was no coincidence that the more radical, formal expressions from the non-western countries were to be found outside the exhibition. This is also true of collections in major western museums: in the Tate you cannot show very complex exhibitions of global modernity in the collection, because you don't have the works to represent this complexity. It will be a long time before Pompidou or the Tate or MoMA will show in a very dialectical, and complex way major modern inventions created in capitals which are not New York, Paris, London, Warsaw or Milan.

If we want to articulate modern proposals from so called non-western cultures and places, we have to discard the syndrome of what I call spontaneous generation, the tendency to present as novelties works which are in fact anchored and articulated within local histories, which have nothing to do with the kind of immediate readings presented in *Les magiciens de la terre*. This is a difficult challenge for curators, because it implies that they have to work in both a retrospective and dialogical manner (what I called "retrospective" in *Documenta X*), and be aware of complex cultural formations, and formal articulations, which is a long process.

This is one of the tasks for curators today: to articulate, while working close to the production of the artist, the complex, sometimes conflicting immediate contemporaneity of diverse works. In a way, the megalopolitan model helps with this task. This model offers a kaleidoscope of histories, representations, and strategies of dealing with images and texts. The French political philosopher Etienne Balibar remarked, after a long tour of the last Documenta, that we will have to learn from the collapse of three illusions of bourgeois culture. The first illusion is the illusion of eternity, which is that art possesses an eternal value that doesn't change. The second is the illusion of evidence, signifying that the esthetic impact is something transcendental, coming from the sky or from the moon, when in fact it is articulated and constructed within a specific cultural formation. The third illusion is that of ubiquity which is that a work will never be the same here and then. And here we could reach a temporary conclusion about art which has great consequences for contemporary curatorship: a work is always the collection of its appearances, there is no such thing as a work forever, no such thing as a heritage cast in stone.

Iwona Blazwick and Catherine David

Debate

Valentijn Byvanck

The audience has heard two very different presentations, each reflecting a particular museum type and curatorial practice. Blazwick's presentation revealed the kind of long-term, wide-ranging, scholarly approach that seems to be the prerogative of large, rich and successful institutions. David's presentation emphasized the significance of "interventions," radical strategies that seem to belong to small, vanguard institutions. My question to Iwona Blazwick, who has just become director of the Whitechapel Gallery, is whether she will embark on staging the kind of strategic event that David just advocated. And more generally, to what extent does the type of institution dictate the program?

Iwona Blazwick

I think that the experience of setting up an institution that didn't exist before, the Tate Modern, will inform my work in Whitechapel. Whitechapel is perhaps unique in the sense that it is such a defined community, unlike for example the institution where I used to work, the Institute for Contemporary Art (ICA), whose neighbors were Buckingham Palace, the Queen, and the Civil Service. The ICA is slightly contextless, whereas for centuries the Whitechapel has been attracting the dispossessed, the exiles, the refugees, the asylum-seekers, and it is a place that, because of its poverty, welcomed and embraced the Jews who had fled the anti-Semitic pogroms of the late nineteenth century, and before them the Huguenots who had fled France in the seventeenth century, right down to the Bengali and Somali population, who find some way of living there today. Whitechapel is thus flanked on the one side by the poor, and highly diverse and interesting cultural groups, and on the other side by that fabulous square mile of the City, which features a very different corporate community. The question of how one represents the audience becomes very challenging; I now have the chance to develop strategies based on my experience with the Tate. The other thing I want to take with me is seeing the present in the context of the past. It has been a revelation to me to work with a collection. Despite the fact that it is primarily white, western and male, it offers a huge richness and vast possibilities of understanding that art is part of continuity, that it doesn't erupt from nowhere but is embedded in traditions and counter-traditions. Then there is the experience of an exhibition named *Central City*, which was addressing what Catherine David called multiple modernisms; looking at synchronisms between Rio de Janeiro and New York in the 1950's, we came to realize that not New York was the birthplace of modernism with the rest of the world following, but that multiple modernisms were happening, almost oblivious of each other. This thought will tell you what I am doing in the Whitechapel, on a micro-scale. Whitechapel does not have a collection, only temporary programs. One of the challenges I will be facing, a pragmatic detail, is that despite our ambitions and desire to look at our history, and to look at it from a global perspective, it is becoming almost impossible to borrow works for exhibitions. Museums regard their collections as assets, and indeed, so do private collectors. The other thing I want is to have a dialogue with cultural productions by commissioning artists to make new works. It's a space with the capacity for that, to help in creating artworks. Whitechapel ought to become something of a hub, and also work in dynamic partnership with other Kunsthalle-type of spaces, from Rio to America to Europe. In Whitechapel we can be more reactive: museums work with very distant deadlines, they schedule programs five years ahead. At Whitechapel we can work much faster.

Valentijn Byvanck

Catherine David suggested that it was really important to show integrity towards artists, by anchoring their work in a local political situation. Don't you need a bigger institution with more historical expertise to do just that? Isn't there some tension between the ambition and small means of small institutions?

Catherine David

I think it is a big problem for both large and small institutions, unless we change the rules. Gallery Lafayette in Paris shows something new every three months. This is one aspect of the problem. Another aspect is the multiplication of exhibitions. Large cities with a lot of power, in terms of both money and of ideas for producing and offering, are over-offering: the talent surpasses the local possibility of confrontation. When that happens you have to opt for institutional implosion, or another way of functioning.

The quantity of shows can be diminished, their rhythm slowed down, perhaps more should be organized outside the institution, another form of commissioning artists and a more diverse program. Some of the projects that fit these descriptions have little to do with exhibitions. So what do we do? Is it not questionable to keep institutions running as before when the exhibitions are no longer challenging? Should one not seek other forms of programming or display? Sometimes you have to come to the point of deciding whether to keep the institution open, or temporarily close it, or to completely change the kinds of activity in the institution. The exchange with the Whitechapel's immediate social surroundings is not necessarily the answer to this problem. One exhibition after another is not the answer. Without transforming the Whitechapel into a kindergarten or in a studio of course – studios are everywhere – the question is: what kind of activity should we focus on, and what kind of event should be organized? Activities and events are two different moments. Activity signals the moment at which you try to put things together and discuss problems. Activities are largely invisible or marginalized, due to the types of production this society favors, and yet I am convinced that they can be profitable to a certain type of audience. Back to the earlier question, I think it is dangerous when institutions like MoMA, Beaubourg, or the Tate are no longer able to invest in long-term research projects, focusing instead solely on transporting and circulating blockbuster shows. Research is crucial, because contemporary practices are not only short-term, immediate things.

Iwona Blazwick

The great benefit of having a collection, something which is manifest, stable and grown, is that you can embark on deep research. Scholars do; they spend their entire careers studying and understanding, from lots of different perspectives, an artist's work, a phenomenon or a material. And that is actually the hidden work of museums, and a very valuable aspect of something static and permanent. With Kunsthalle-type or temporary exhibition spaces, the pressures of programming spectacle, the fact that it is flying past, one thing after another in a kind of industrial way, makes in-depth research much more difficult. But also, I think, this pace does allow different relations with processes. One sees it, one can understand it much more fluidly, in an on-going way, and the challenge for me will be to harness, within the convention of gallery spaces, inside this building with its distinctive architectural features, a new way of understanding cultural production. And then to find conditions of both experience and interpretation with which one can address all these different publics which are our neighbors, and which shape our context.

Valentijn Byvanck

Is this the difference between the old and the new curator? The former engaged in deep research and delving into the collections of the museums; the latter scouting for new esthetic practices and, without interrupting the flow of things, targeting specific audiences with these practices?

Iwona Blazwick

I don't think so. One of the great joys of the Tate's collections is the Internet archive, an extraordinary resource that is available to everybody, and I would encourage everyone here to visit it. The archive has one of the greatest collections of Fluxus, which originally wasn't even admitted to the library collection. About this group, which has vanished without a trace, you can find out who was producing what, at what stage of history they were, and what the canon has become. I'm sad to have left that, I must say. The great relevance of working with permanent collections is that one comes to understand the histories, and as a result one can question the canon: to me, that is a very dynamic and contemporary relevant process.

Audience

Are you not afraid that these Tate groupings lead to a rather schematic and static representation of art? Where, for instance, do you place Duchamp's ready-mades?

Iwona Blazwick

That was a big issue for us. Where do you put ready-mades in an evolutionary or linear model? Many figures resist that model. Where do you put Malevich, where black monograms? Duchamp or Joseph Beuys can be situated in all four of these categories; we find new meaning and new understanding in each category. And that is absolutely intrinsic to our approach: it is a temporary framework and one that is completely contingent. The categories itself are a kind of classification, which is art-historically established and then exploded, but it provided us with a way of trying to organize subject-matter. And the provocation and the resistances against this are as interesting to us as the things which are more easily definable and categorizable. We wanted to do something and than perhaps disturb it, turn it upside down. It's there to be challenged.

Audience

Could Catherine David say a bit more about staging events? The framework of museums, or even the Documenta seems insufficient: what is the alternative?

Catherine David

When I use the phrase "staging events," I mean to de-emphasize the idea of an exhibition and stress the possibility of alternative models. Sometimes the esthetic practice lies in redesigning the space, in trying to put together a design of a structure, or it lies in discursive rather than visual elements. Choosing the right form and right medium is very difficult. At the moment I am working on a project about contemporary Arab representations. Proposals come from different cultural actors – I prefer the term actor to artist. Some works can be hung on the wall, others are moving images, or performances, and still others are part of an operation which I cannot temporarily stop so a discursive presentation might be the best format. There are many ways. At the Hundred Days of the Documenta, the point was to make the audience understand that this space was for discussion, confrontation, for discursive elements, that the space was sometimes activated by real bodies, real discourse, and sometimes it was without activity, but then one still had access to the sedimentation of discourses and actions that had taken place there earlier. There was a minimal staging of events. In the project about contemporary Arab representations, it will be more complex. It is a much smaller event than the Documenta, and too many interferences would destroy its sophistication.

Iwona Blazwick

I would also like to emphasize that all this time I have been living and working in the city of London, a highly pro-active metropolis. And at times you want the opposite, you want something which is very static, very anchored and still, and which will immerse you not in a progression of time and space, but in a state of complete stillness where you can take yourself around an object. I think that sometimes the context of a city or a space can make you desire different things. Slow or deep experiences, fast-moving, unfolding experiences. For example, the earth-room Walter de Maria made for the Dia Foundation in New York is very monolithic in grandiose terms; nonetheless, for me it's hugely pleasurable to go there, to another pro-active metropolis, and find a room full of earth. And it will be there for many years. I must say I get a deep sense of pleasure visiting it occasionally. One must be able to offer all these different kinds of experiences.

Catherine David

I agree with you, except that I think we shouldn't confuse – and I think it happens quite often – a very complex editing, which means mixing different individualities, with a *kinotage permanent,* a rapid succession of shows, which for me is not a very desirable exhibition mode. Another thing you mention is that sometimes, of course, you need to see a video for two hours. How can you stage such an event without giving the visitor the frustrating feeling that he is either too early or too late?

Audience

Artists always have to deal with the viewpoint of curators; are those not very different from those of artists?

Iwona Blazwick

Well, certainly in terms of subjectivity: I come from a feminist position, and I was very aware that working in Tate Modern my sensibility was more or less invisible. And the identity and representation of white western males certainly shaped the way we were trying to look at the collection: we were trying to understand what was missing, as well as amplify what was there. And I think that's another kind of issue for big institutions; how do audiences seek their own experiences represented in the exhibitions and programs? I'm going off the point here – one of the interesting things was how the audience changed when we were showing the work of Chris Ofili and Steve McQueen. It was very clear – for the first time, actually –, that the Afro-Caribbean, or West-Indian constituencies, which are very much part of the London audiences, decided to come. Because for the first time, they could find two artists who showed *their* reality. And that is a very important issue, both in terms of identification and representation.

Audience

Often curators focus their attention on the big places, and famous art schools, at the expense of artists who work in distant and unfashionable locations, smaller institutions, and for lesser-known audiences. Do you visit these places?

Catherine David

Of course, up to a point. In the context of the project about contemporary Arab representations I would love to go to Yemen, but that is not always possible. I completely agree with you that the contemporary mappings of esthetical production could be more nuanced, less mainstream. Many things are happening outside the big centers, and yet many curators choose to stay within the confines of those centers. If you go to Beirut, you might discover interesting things, but if you expect to find New York there, you might be disappointed: one should not look for Paris in Dakar. And the point is not only to go: in the last five years, curators have found a lot of exotic, new destinations, but the question is what one is doing there. It would be very easy to collect some artists in Beirut and bring them to Paris, and it would be very exciting, very aggressive. But it is probably much more meaningful and responsible to contribute to the consolidation of a very interesting location than to dislocate for immediate circulation, without distance, productions which require other paradigms.

Iwona Blazwick

It's a really difficult question. We can't be cyclopedic, you can't just travel around the world like a butterfly-collector. I have to depend on signals. In Glasgow, for example, a group of artists formed a gallery called Transmission, and this name is very important. Because of its program – it is a small gallery – it became a sort of powerhouse of activity, you just *had* to go there. They made it their business to tell the world that they were there. And once you knew, you got on that train to go and see what was happening. Do you know what I mean? You can't just say: I'm off to Glasgow, Senegal or wherever. There must be a reason. And also for me the journey is always precipitated by something, a rumor, a piece of paper, a clue, an artist saying something, and then you follow up the lead. I think there have been wonderful moments, for example, I was working in Antwerp in 1993, when it was European Capital of Culture, and I found out that between 1968 to 1974 there had been an incredible proliferation of artist-spaces, where artists worked who are now canonical figures, but who at that time were unknown, like Marcel Broodthaers, Laurence Wiener and Carl Andre. They all came to these spaces, and worked there, the American artists had no support from their country, no scholarships, and they went to Nova Scotia, to Halifax, really out-of-the-way places, because there was somebody who gave them a space, gave them some money, there was a belief and a point of confluence. I think the idea of artists communicating in a group, supporting each other, a kind of critical moment, the nascent moment, seems to set a light on certain locations, and then stories come from there and you can start to find out things. There have been these wonderful crosscurrents, exchanges, and cross-fertilization. From a curatorial standpoint, the challenge is how to find them, why do you go to these places, what do you expect, what are your criteria, and how do you translate and interpret what you find, and show it in a different context. These are big questions.

IV. Art and Design

Anthony Dunne
Fiona Raby
Alan Murray

Foreword

Design is viewed as one of the hot new niches of the visual arts. Modern art museums launch big shows about contemporary design, and designer products are increasingly perceived as art. In the wake of these developments, the art world is becoming aware of areas in which designers and artists work on projects that cannot be defined as either art or design. Anthony Dunne and Fiona Raby, both on the research and teaching staff of the Royal College of Art in London, work in one of those areas.

In 1999 they published *Hertzian Tales*, a refreshing look at the new possibilities and problems of "intelligent" design for an electronically sophisticated but otherwise conventional society.[1] Modern life is dominated by intelligent machines and advanced technology. Designers are usually the guardians of this development: they operate electronic amenities with smart gadgets and protect the consumer from the dilemmas they cause. Dunne and Raby counteract this role by advocating critical design that actually creates new dilemmas and addresses the dark side of modern existence. In their new publication *Design Noir*, they call on designers to create a world of electronic objects in which standardization is shunned and where there is room for "danger, adventure and transgression."[2] Artist Alan Murray of the industrial design department at the Eindhoven Institute of Technology responds critically to their call. In his opinion, Dunne and Raby's project is less a case of radical design than of "light entertainment."

The debate, titled *Design Noir*, took place on November 27, 2001, and was prompted by the appearance of the eponymous publication. Earlier that year Dunne and Raby had presented their work *Placebo: Compass Room* in the exhibition *Breeze of AIR/Hortus Conclusus* at Witte de With.

1. Anthony Dunne, *Hertzian Tales: Electronic Products, Aesthetic Experience and Critical Design* (London: RCA CRD Research Publications, 1999).
2. Anthony Dunne and Fiona Raby, *Design Noir: The Secret Life of Electronic Objects* (Basel: Birkhäuser, 2002).

Anthony Dunne and Fiona Raby

Design Noir

Fiona Raby is an architect and I am an industrial designer. About ten years ago, after leaving college, we moved to Japan. We were hoping, rather idealistically, to work with technological systems in order to create better products, services, environments – and we were thoroughly disappointed. I worked for Sony, designing plastic casings. Since I was concentrating solely on the semiotic husks of gadgets, I never had the opportunity to think about the technology itself, or to question our relationship to it. Meanwhile Fiona was working at a radical design and architecture studio, where we both became involved in hi-tech installations, but this was also dissatisfying. The main reason was that when you work with installations, people tend to pigeonhole you.

Three years later we returned to London and set up our own studio to develop our ideas and explore new technologies. We also started teaching at the Royal College of Art, which was then setting up a new department called Computer Related Design. We became founding members of the department's Research Studio, and have been there now for over seven years. The studio has thirteen researchers – artists, designers, psychologists – all preoccupied, in different ways, with looking at technology from a more cultural perspective.

Our own goal is to open up a kind of critical angle on how technology expresses itself through products and services. So we are interested in the role of designers in an academic context. We aim to develop design proposals – less prototypes than concepts in tangible form – and to present them in a way that promotes debate. In that sense, our methodology is related to that of much fine art practice, being essentially about provocation and ambiguity. But it's crucial to us that our work is perceived as *design*. Industrial designers, if they are not designing things to be manufactured for a mass market, are often marginalized. Their work is seen as somehow fictional, as "arty" (meaning self-indulgent or escapist). It's seen as anything but design. Yet design is precisely the space within which we operate, in an effort to connect with many different audiences, to raise awareness of critical issues, to stimulate discussion.

Recently there was a trial in America about the use of infrared imaging. During surveillance of someone's home, the police had pointed a heat registration device at the house next door, and the thing went right off the scale. Naturally the police were suspicious. They obtained the electricity bill and discovered that this house was consuming vast amounts of power. On searching the place, they found roomfuls of marijuana plants growing under high-intensity lights. In court, the owner of the house argued that the police had unlawfully invaded his home with their radiation device, while the police argued that the man's home had "leaked" onto the street. This controversy caused lengthy debate; finally the court ruled in favor of the police: the heat had leaked through the walls into the public domain. The rationale was that the police didn't invade the man's privacy, as they would have done if they had used a measuring device which passes through walls, such as an x-ray.

I mention this simply as an introduction to the area of design that fascinates us: the redefinition of our environment to include the electromagnetic spectrum, and the resultant blurring of notions of what it means to be "inside" and "outside." Most people regard the electromagnetic environment as forbiddingly technical. Actually, the difficulty in understanding it has less to do with technical expertise than with sheer complexity. This space consists of a huge set of different interconnected energies. At one end of the spectrum, there are the low frequency waves emitted by wiring. Then there are the radio waves emitted by televisions, radios (long and short wave), telephones, microwaves, and so on. Then comes infrared, a form of light we can't see with our eyes but do feel on our skin. At the far end of the spectrum, there are ultraviolet rays and x-rays.

All the physical objects that emit such electromagnetic radiation are interconnected in an environment we choose to call Hertzian space – "space," because it is not just a medium for broadcasting information, or a way of doing without wiring, but is something we *inhabit*. When viewed at the frequency of light (that is, with the naked eye), objects stop at their edges. But if you tune up the spectrum a little, the objects continue to expand, interpenetrating each other and our own bodies. They create a space around them, commingling with other electromagnetic spaces, through which we move.

To help people grasp this idea, British Telecom created a computer model showing the waves of a cellular phone transmitter moving through a series of buildings. This demonstration was effective because the waves weren't illustrative, weren't merely diagrammatic. These were the actual waves, made visible. Here was a tiny portion of the Hertzian landscape. Normally we can't sense it at all, and yet it's all around us – it's *inside* us. This is the landscape we are designing for. How should we inhabit it? How should we relate to it? Which parts are dangerous, and which pleasurable? What might such dangers and pleasures mean?

With radio and television, and radar, and the proliferation of cellular phones, it is becoming increasingly difficult to find non-electronic spaces – meaning, spaces with no electrical charge. Virtually the whole globe is an intense soup of radiation. Yet nobody is doing anything about it. We have no idea if it is harmful or not.

This observation gave rise to our interest in electromagnetic shielding. Perhaps people need to retreat into their own electronic-free, magnetic-free cases. Ideally your whole house would be shielded, but only the privileged few could afford such protection. So we conceived of a more humble object which we called a Faraday Chair: a special box which is earthed and completely electronic- and magnetic-free. It is almost like an antique space.

It's a utilitarian solution – compact, functional and affordable to many. The idea is that you curl up inside it and breathe through a sort of snorkel. The material of the box incorporates a conductor film called data-safe film, which blocks out phones, TVs, all those frequencies. Data-safe film is used in government buildings in Britain, and probably around the world too. Its purpose is to prevent information leaking from computers, so that spies can't simply drive up to a high-security building and tune in. The Faraday Chair was not designed to be manufactured, but to contribute to this debate *as an icon* – an image to circulate, offering a focus for thought.

As should be clear by now, we are concerned with objects that embody values. In fact, we often initiate the design process by considering an interesting cultural problem (social, ethical, moral), and eventually arrive at a solution which solves the practical aspects of the problem in a very direct way. Paradoxically, the result is an object that addresses the wider issues somewhat indirectly, and thus, in our view, quite powerfully. A good example of a such a product – not by us, but inspirational for us – is the Truth Phone.

The Truth Phone looks and operates like an ordinary telephone, but it has a built-in voice stress analyzer. This device purports to indicate the truthfulness of the person you're speaking to. The phone was designed for employers, to intimidate employees, and is a serious piece of technology. It works by picking up the voice tremors which usually – though not always – reflect stress. It doesn't work on pathological liars because they don't think they're lying; it doesn't work on people with a guilt complex, because they always think they're lying; and it doesn't work if someone speaks very erratically. So it has problems as a practical tool. But as a conceptual tool it is enlightening. For us, it provides a way of thinking about the *esthetic* potential of electronic products. I'm not talking about form or material or construction or even interactivity, but about narrative opportunity. Imagine you could rent this phone. You might take it home, plug it in, talk to your mother or your lover – and discover that they're lying. Suddenly you're thrown into a dilemma: do you confront them or do live with it? Either way, your life – your life *story* – will change.

It's a simple design scenario with dramatic social and psychological consequences. We are very drawn to such scenarios and the opportunities they afford for an incisive critique of our emerging electromagnetic culture. By fusing different levels of electronic functionality, we can create all kinds of psychologically charged situations, where ordinary products propel the user into an uncertain world fraught with moral difficulties. Much like a film. And this was one of the starting points for *Design Noir*.

The UK Scanning Directory, published annually, lists every single frequency used in the UK. These frequencies form a sort of real estate, most of which is owned by the government. Only a fraction is open to the general public. Larger portions are available for commercial use, but licenses are astronomically expensive. (Recently mobile phone companies paid huge sums for a slice of the spectrum.) So this super-valuable real estate makes for highly political space.

The first page of the directory says, "This book is designed and compiled purely for entertainment and educational purposes, and is not intended to be used in conjunction with any type or form of VHF/UHF scanning receiver, which may be in direct contravention of the Wireless Telegraphy Act, or as a professional guide." You can buy the scanner. You can buy the book. You can use the scanner to listen to radio stations. But the minute you use it to listen, say, to the police, you're breaking the law ... And if you trade in the information you find out, you can be in jail for several years.

Thus the scanner has a curious status, at the limits of legality. Of course, much of the spectrum is less hazardous for eavesdroppers. There are thousands of harmless frequencies – for small companies, for dog catchers, for tiny radio stations broadcasting in a radius of a few hundred meters. We decided to explore this rich electromagnetic texture by monitoring specific frequencies. The project was called Tuneable Cities, and focused on London.

One of the most intriguing frequencies listed in the book is "illegal bugging devices." We bought a bugging device, legally, for a mere forty pounds. It's a standard electrical socket plug containing a wireless microphone. You simply plug it in somewhere and then tune in elsewhere with a normal radio. The results were incredibly clear. It made us wonder if we could pick up other people's bugs hidden around London. So we put the scanner in our car, tuned into the frequency for illegal bugging devices, and went to the obvious places: the central law courts, the newspaper district, the embassies of Mayfair. At all these locations the scanner clicked, indicating devices nearby. Then, outside a building close to Mayfair, we were amazed to find ourselves listening to noises in a room. We could hear people moving around, cups clinking, snippets of conversation.

Enticed by this discovery, we referred to the book again and selected "babycoms" (baby intercoms). We chose an area called Chiswick, which is full of young families, and ventured out again with our scanner. We drove slowly up and down the streets, mapping the coos and cries of babycoms. After only a few hours, our map was speckled with black dots.

As designers, how do we define these new spaces?

One answer might be to follow the scientific practice of bird-tagging. We could tag birds with little ID radios so that as they fly, they describe the electromagnetic space for us. We could then listen to these "radio birds" in our cars. Most of the time we'd probably get the rustling of static, but once in a while there would be an explosion of sound from a migrating flock.

Our intention wasn't really to design a new car radio. We were more interested in proposing a different logic for design. Rather than cutting off the driver from the outside environment, our radio could radically connect the driver – and not just to radio birds. The radio could have buttons for different types of reception, public and private, so that the driver could choose whether to invade people's privacy. There could be a local button for the immediate vicinity. There could be presets for babycoms, bugging devices, atmospheric radio. There could be a legal/illegal button. And so on. The point is that such choices are often not available to designers, because others decide what is socially acceptable. In this project we wanted to make these decisions ourselves. To be more accurate, we wanted to *not* make these decisions, as far as possible. We were keen to pass on that privilege to the users, to allow our designs to liberate rather than constrain. Let people misuse them at their own discretion.

We also worked on a proposal for a domestic radio that would pick up only what is within fifty meters. The radio would detect mundane activity, like wireless garage door-openers or a neighbor's TV. Our prototype was an inflatable pillow enclosing a fluorescent plastic box with an LCD screen. The pillow automatically tunes to different frequencies, each of which creates a corresponding pattern on the LCD: pulsing dots, jiggling squares, a swirl of diamonds. It's interactive, too. When you wave a hand around the pillow, you change the pattern. But the main idea is that you gradually learn which patterns correspond to which frequencies, so that, for example, you see that someone nearby is using a mobile phone. But you can also hear the transmissions, if you listen closely. When you rest your head on the pillow at night, you might hear the buzz of a fax machine, or two lovers exchanging telephonic sweet nothings.

We placed our prototype in an exhibition, *Monitor as Material*, but this was disappointing. Visitors responded to the pillow as a piece of art, not as a potential product. They reacted to the context, rather than asking themselves what it might be like to *live* with such a thing. As a result, we started to consider how electronic products function in everyday life and how people relate to them. In other words, we moved a step further away from thinking about the objects themselves. More and more, we found that the practice of critical design leads to a greater curiosity – even wonder – about people.

We worked with a film student, Dan Sellars, on a fake documentary. In this documentary we wanted to create what we call "value fiction" – fiction that employs technical realism to challenge cultural values.

The film shows us approaching a conventional elderly lady called Olive who lives alone. She regularly uses the scanner and pillow, and we interview her about this. Olive enthuses about the pillow, explaining that it is a significant part of her life, and that she often uses it in the garden because the reception seems better in her wooden summer house. She obtained it by chance, from a friend who ordered it from the back of a magazine and then lost interest.

But Olive would never give it away. In fact, just the other day she was telling a neighbor about it, and now the neighbor keeps asking to borrow it ... Olive's fictional anecdotes gave a fresh perspective on how electronic products circulate in society, and how they are actually used. And the ways that people project their lives onto these products was the point of departure for our most recent project, Placebo, in which we worked with technology outside the context of a gallery.

In creating Placebo furniture, our primary aim was to provoke others into revealing their fears and hopes about Hertzian space. We also wanted to see how people would feel about living with conceptual objects – devices which are neither entirely utilitarian, nor strictly art. Would they be uncomfortable with such an ambiguous mix of the poetic and the prosaic? Or would they send our objects straight back to the gallery? Of course, people are used to the idea of electronic products, but even here there was mystery. Beyond the glossy surface of magazines, beyond the bright shop windows, the official life of these products ends. What goes on at home? How do all the gadgets relate to each other? What about the *secret* life of electronic products?

Our designs were very schematic. We were keen to minimize the semiotic load of the furniture, leaving users free to read their own meanings into them. The result was plain wooden chairs and tables, each containing an unobtrusive electronic device. Having made them, we sought "adopters" to live with them. By way of advertising, we displayed the objects in a window of Selfridges, a big department store in the middle of London (which was showing work by us and other designers in the run-up to a major prize). We included our phone number and fifty people rang, most of whom knew little about design. We sent these people adoption forms asking them to state which object they wanted to adopt, and why. We also asked if their own electronic products had ever misbehaved, or whether they were worried about electromagnetic waves. Had they had any previous electromagnetic experiences? This last question was meaningless. We were just interested to see what people would make of it, how imaginative they were. Eventually we narrowed our selection down to eight families and groups – a mixture of young and old, couples and singles.

One of our designs is called the Nipple Chair. In the back it has two small sensors – nipples – which pick up electromagnetic radiation occurring in the room and passing through your body. If you're sitting on the chair in the field of radiation, the nipples vibrate. Someone working at a computer might feel the vibration and decide to stop, or they might enjoy the experience. As it turned out, our adopter more than enjoyed it. He said that the slight noise of the nipples was quite different to listening to the fridge. "It's a nice background. Sometimes I try to use my brain to change the rate of the vibration. Of course I can't, but I keep trying." He added, "When I come home at night, it does start to speed up [because of static in his body] and I think it's pleased to see me, although I know it isn't."

This person loved gadgets, so we asked him if the Nipple Chair *was* a gadget. He thought it was a special kind of gadget that wasn't "gadget-like," since you couldn't adjust it in any way – but that was exactly what he liked about it. In short, he wanted to control it and yet he enjoyed its implacability; and he wanted it to respond to his behavior, and yet enjoyed its inscrutability. But his ambivalence is best expressed in his own words, in this fascinating comment: "Can something be a gadget and be esthetic as well? And can its function as a gadget be more esthetic than the object itself?"

Another Placebo design is the GPS Table – a table with a global positioning sensor inside it. The sensor can display its geographical position only when it has an unobstructed link to a particular satellite. So it has to be placed by a large window, or in a garden. Otherwise it indicates that it is lost. This message drew strong reactions from the couple who adopted the GPS Table. Dick said, "When I first plugged it in and it said 'lost,' I was shocked. I'm not quite sure why. I just thought: Oh, the poor thing!" And, since that first day, his "affection" had steadily grown for this enigmatic object.

And yet the table became more than a focus for unlikely endearment. Lorna was also struck by the humbling experience of finding herself connected to a cosmic network and sensing that she was merely one point on one planet. Thus the table transcended its initial status as a mundane object and became the instrument of a metaphysical perspective.

We love the idea that everyday objects can make you think, and can provoke strong emotions. All our adopters also believed that there is a place for things that combine utilitarian and creative qualities, the functional and the reflective. However, when we presented the Placebo furniture to designers, they said it was art, not design. And manufacturers said there was no market for such products.

We agree. There is no market, yet. There's no need for a table with a global positioning system, or a chair with electromagnetic sensors. But once people start living with these things, *then* they feel the need. Then they tell you that everybody should have one.

Alan Murray

Reply

I taught at the Design Academy, Eindhoven, for two years before moving to the Technical University in the same city to start a department of "Entertainment" within the new faculty of Industrial Design. As an artist, I have been predominantly rewriting and designing instruction manuals and user guides.

I started rewriting instruction manuals when I was still at art school. My typical studio activity was to test products such as a Krupps espresso coffee machine. Part of my enjoyment at the time was to confound some of my teachers. A typical "discovery" for the week might be that in the coffee machine instruction manual it says to pour one liter of water into the coffee machine. In fact its glass carafe would only hold 0.75 liters of coffee (so 0.25 liters would always spill out). I liked the idea of confrontation through a very applied approach. Although this was initially a thrill-seeking foray into another discipline, it has developed into an artists practice in which it is wholly reasonable to work for three years on a guide to the game of squash and exhibit it as art. Those using the guide-to-squash do not know it is an artwork, nor do they need to know. It functions on the one hand as an excellent model of sport communication and on the other as an investigation into the possible role and approach of an artist. I feel it has superseded the initial typical "flavor" of a user-guide into actually being one.

In juxtaposition, I can imagine that designers such as Anthony Dunne and Fiona Raby might find the traditional approach of an artist very attractive. When a designer's norm has been to design with a "happy ever after" approach, the seeming freedom with which an artist indulgently confronts an audience with objects that cannot be explained immediately must be extremely intriguing. This dilemma is what Dunne and Raby find so interesting.

Unlike design, that focuses on questions including, what is it, how does it function, and what should I do with it, art allows for the exploration of more ambiguous questions. Indeed, great dilemmas have helped revolutionize and re-position art, constantly urging people to rethink what art is, and where and why it should exist. Duchamp's work exemplifies this process. And so does Mathew Barney's; it weaves a narrative of dilemmas, spellbinding an audience.

With their work and writings, Dunne and Raby call for a Design Revolution. But they already walk a tightrope of compromises. On the one hand they are calling for an "embedded wickedness that will truly make the user a protagonist and co-producer of narrative experience, rather than a passive consumer of a product's meaning." On the other hand, they propose a scheme that treads a very reasonable path through the middle ground of confrontation. In their design, they emphasize "slight strangeness;" when objects are "too weird," they are "instantly dismissed," when they are "not strange enough, they are absorbed into everyday reality." In light of their statement to develop "alternative and often gently provocative artifacts which set out to engage people through humor, insight, surprise and wonder," their level of confrontation must be characterized as mild.

This is not the confrontational "recipe" of an artist. An artist's confrontation might veer towards the uncomfortable, painful, unexplainable or monumental. I feel Dunne and Raby are instead proposing a "mildly entertaining" design platform from which a designer can amuse and titillate, evoke a giggle rather than a cry, create a comfortable zone of elegant game-playing where a user can engage with the design object and never fear what ultimate consequences that engagement might have.

Anthony Dunne, Fiona Raby and Alan Murray

Debate

Valentijn Byvanck

Tony Dunne and Fiona Raby, perhaps you wish to respond to Alan Murray's comments.

Anthony Dunne

I think the point of the relative extremism of art is well taken. Most designers are told to create for themselves a demographic picture for each product: what is the median age of the consumer, what is his lifestyle, what kind of market is it? This is a very abstract model of normality. Instead, we're suggesting that designers look to more extreme people, not as models to be employed, or to be transformed into ordinary people, but as a source of inspiration to look at and to be excited by. In addition, I agree our form of subversion is mild. That is intentional: we do not want to alienate, or project ourselves into a space which is much better occupied by artists, but to participate – maybe on the edges – to have some kind of dialogue, to extend the situation. Concerning Murray's comment about entertainment: we believe that humor is very important. We are not utopian: we don't believe you can dramatically change reality. But we don't drop out either. People expect critical things to be serious, but we believe that things can be critical and optimistic. It is not about preaching, it is about offering something in an interesting and engaging way. We never rallied for a revolution, but it is certainly our aim to encourage designers to rethink the ways in which they work, to question their models of reference. We aim at opening things up and then seeing what comes out.

Audience

Weren't you afraid that by using the word adoption, you would predetermine the effect that the GPS table would have on people?

Anthony Dunne

That is a good point. It is a loaded word. Yet, it made it easier to place these objects. Our nightmare was that we show up with these objects and people don't see the point of it. Some had applied on the basis of descriptions they had read, others had seen them, but none had actually touched or experienced the objects. We feared a situation in which the applicants would ring us up two days later and say: please take these boring objects away.

Alan Murray

When you use the world "lost" in a table, you load the bet towards you. The worst thing for you is that people say: this is boring, we don't want it. From my point of view, if people would find it boring, I would find that quite interesting. I wonder if this loading of the chances won't effect negatively the level of response. When I look at your objects, they don't seem abstract at all, instead they look like design objects that people would immediately talk about as art objects. If the compass would have been in a table that would have been more invisible, maybe the reaction would have been different, but these objects stuck out like sore thumbs in people's interiors.

Audience

Speaking about adoption: did you ever take it away?

Anthony Dunne

We miscalculated taking things away. That was a part of the design process we completely neglected. Everyone knew we were going to collect these objects, but when it happened half of the people were very disappointed.

Valentijn Byvanck

In your presentation, the objects seem to serve predominantly one function, they offer an outlet for affective behavior. Is that not a disappointing outcome when you set out to open up a field to all kinds of new design functions?

Anthony Dunne

With each object, you can see extra functionalities. One of the things we were concerned about in our previous work: we had built completely new kinds of objects, with a complex functionality, and people found it hard to connect with them. We had to explain again and again how the object worked. So we decided to strip them down, simplify the range of functions. And from here on, we can start to diversify again, because I agree that other layers of functionality would make things more interesting.

Audience

The GPS table seems more a story than a function.

Anthony Dunne

Yes, in that particular one the information counts, not the technology. That is in itself already an interesting observation. One of the reasons that you don't often see technology and furniture combined is that the furniture becomes redundant the moment its technology has become obsolete. What's interesting with the GPS is that its information doesn't ever really become obsolete; one cannot replace the object with one that has an upgraded technology, or a better sensor. We wanted to be able to look at these issues in a kind of abstract way and purposefully strip down the objects to help us figure out what's going on.

Fiona Raby

In our presentation tonight we only discussed electronic objects which had some kind of autonomous behavior. There were six other objects which had no kind of electronic function. People got attached to these objects for different reasons. For instance, we had a square with pink foam attached to it and we told people that it absorbs electromagnetic radiation, and if you put it between you and an electronic object, it would protect them from the radiation. We explained to them that the protection is conceptual rather than technical, that is, it was a placebo. The adopter Lauren wanted the object because her boyfriend Jan was a musician who had a recording studio in their spare bedroom. The room was filled with equipment – speakers, computer, modem – which he refused to switch of. She was terrified of all the electronic radiation and wanted to protect herself from it. Jan told her that the pink foam was a ridiculous object that would never protect her. But for her, it became a symbolic kind of protection. Yet, it also made her aware of all the electronic things in her bedroom – the hairdryer, the mobile phone charger – and she became paranoid. This was a totally unexpected response. We never thought that anyone would revaluate their home because of the object. Nor did we foresee the various uses people would put the objects to. Lauren not only used the foam against Jan's equipment, she also put it in between her and the television. In addition, they were talking about hanging it on the wall like a work of art. This is an example of the territory we're operating in. We want to see if little changes in our every day materiality can create profound ideas. Lorna felt that the GPS table connected her to satellites. It pulled her out of her everyday experience of being a housewife and looking after her child. And for us that tiny bit of subversion was a big success. You don't have to go to a gallery to be entertained, you can have something at home that touches you. That is not necessarily poetic, it can also be profound.

Alan Murray

Somewhere in your book you talked about science fiction, having imaginative objects in a conservative culture, and you put forward this idea of value-fiction as an alternative way of critical design, where you say: well, we use everyday objects, to heighten the cultural imagination. This everyday profundity reminded me of artists that run to a gallery with the proof that they do something in the real world. I've done it so many times myself: a project stirs up people, you receive a letter from someone and you feel that you tipped something in the real world. Subsequently, you put it on the art gallery wall to tell the world that you touched something in the real world. And in a way, it is not the profound difference that you made, but the appreciation of your value fiction that is most important. This feeling is reinforced by the way you photographed your objects in the book; the photo's are very beautiful, and very moody, in a fashion magazine style, which makes it seem as if the people were fodder for your value fiction.

Anthony Dunne

Science fiction seems to paint a picture of the future, where we would have all these sorts of technologies, but it turns out that we still live in the same way, with the same gender and social stereotypes. What we are trying to suggest is that you take the technologies around us, whether it is radios, sensors, compasses, or a conductive pink foam, and by combining those in different ways, living objects would come out that aren't futuristic, but form an alternative now. We didn't want to valuate the objects. Nor was it our intention to attract attention to the fact that we're connecting with real people, or the real world. Instead, we are genuinely interested in seeing how people, once we gave these objects away, lived with them. We would have learned a lot too, if people had rejected them. Yet at the end of the day we are designers, and there is a side to us that tries to shape things. These are artificial objects, they're kind of experimental, designed in a very abstract way.

They are design objects, that is their context. Yet, most designers condemn these projects. Their view of design is about shape, style, material, about the way objects are manufactured or marketed. None of our objects have these things associated with it. We wanted to be clear that they are not products, they are just devices to slip into peoples homes. They have an esthetic that makes them semi-there, not real, robust products. They are wrought with all sorts of contradictions and complexities, but that's what we enjoy, taking a position and trying things out.

Fiona Raby

An endless number of tables and chairs are manufactured which exemplify the fact that designing is most of the time just a process of reshaping material and form. Function is not a subject of discussion. And that's our point: we're making a relation to design beyond looking at shape and style. Instead, we think about the role objects play in everyday life. As to your comment about the photography, we did work with a fashion photographer, who sat in on the interview, the rule being that the pictures had to reflect what people said, be more than mere documentation. Fashion photographers are used to working with people, they are able to make people feel very comfortable without having to tidy up the house. That was a pragmatic choice.

Audience

Is there a certain agenda you have for the projects in everyday life, or is everything allowed?

Anthony Dunne

We work as researchers. Although we have to get external funding for our work and find people to support it, we do things you couldn't do in a company, a design consultancy, or as a freelance independent designer. We are not interested in manufacturing it. We hope companies look at our work and get interested in this softer, more modest way of presenting technology in the home. It may generate a set of products that fit a different way of thinking. People are so unbelievably carefree about this invisible environment that's taking shape, with its side-products and radiation. In England, the government allocates only a tiny amount of money, last year 300,000 pounds, for researching the effects of mobile phones; no one really knows whether this stuff is harmful or not. When you do come across literature, it's usually highly technical. We're interested in introducing, through design, this kind of awareness into people's homes. From a public standpoint, we aim to cause more awareness and discussion about the presence of these invisible fields. Not in an alarming way, in which people panic, nor in a naive way: oh we can make everything wireless and connect everything up. In addition, we have an agenda aimed at designers, which says: look, these things are very simple, why can't we have objects that offer more interesting esthetic or psychological experiences, why not encourage a more conceptual kind of relationship? What's holding it back, marketing? Production? Design ideology? As academics, working in a university setting, we don't have to put our works into production or find a manufacturer. Instead, we see it as our task to push the limits of design, to extend the space, to experiment.

Alan Murray

In an interview I once said my work was on the verge of being a moral nightmare. Can you say the same about your work?

Fiona Raby

Yes, we work on the edges of industry and commercialization, everything we produce, can be commercialized and consumed, especially the stuff with mobile phones can be easily hijacked purely for selling purposes. And that's a problem in many of our projects; when we open up a space for people to think in a new social way, there is always the danger that it can be used to sell more things.

V. Non-Western Art

Janneke Wesseling

Charlotte Huygens

Kitty Zijlmans

Els van der Plas

Foreword

In the summer of 2000 an intriguing conflict took place in Rotterdam's museum world. With its permanent presentation featuring Rotterdam immigrant families, the World Arts Museum had incurred the wrath of the Historical Museum, which claimed that the presentation belonged in its own institution. "The World Museum should concern itself with the world," declared the director of the Historical Museum, "Rotterdam is our business."[1] His claim triggered a battery of accusations. Museum Boijmans Van Beuningen, for instance, was charged with encroaching upon another museum's territory since it had staged an exhibition of Moroccan pottery. Confronted with a neighbors' squabble that had got out of hand, Rotterdam's commissioner of cultural affairs Hans Kombrink declared that he would not subsidize overlapping collections and exhibition territories and ordered the institutions to consider demarcating their borders. In adopting this stance, Kombrink trained the political spotlights on a problem that has been preoccupying the museum world for some time: the development of identity in a new social order.[2] Blurred interdisciplinary borders, the new historical curriculum and the search for a new global order have been prompting museums to reconsider their profile in recent years. Non-western art is an important cause and catalyst in this development. All institutions have to adopt a stance in one way or another.

In this context Witte de With organized two debates on the place of non-western art in western institutions. Non-western art is eagerly exhibited, and to a lesser extent collected, by Dutch art institutions and subsidized by various government agencies and funds. Swept along on the current of globalization and migration, the genre is prompting a series of complex questions about western museum practice, expertise and classification. In addition, it raises questions about the relationship between art and society. What is the political agenda behind collecting and displaying non-western art? What is its place within the western art canon? And what is the critic's role in the dissemination of non-western art?

1. *Rotterdams Dagblad*, April 22, 2000.

2. On the underlying causes of this border conflict see Valentijn Byvanck, "*Het museum moet een tweede leven worden gegund*" [the museum must be granted a second life], published under the heading "*De muffe museumgeur verdrijven met eigentijdse programmering*" [blow away the stale museum air with contemporary programming], *Museumvisie*, no. 4 (2001/2002): 29-31.

The subject has led to frequent discussions about the quality of non-western art and the accuracy of the distinction between western and non-western. Here, those questions were avoided as far as possible. Not because they are unimportant, but because in the first place they tend to get bogged down in a deadlock between two or more classes of taste, and in the second place they pass over the fact that separating western from non-western, theoretically correct or not, informs the practice and perspective of most museums, funds, governments, and even scholarship. The speakers were therefore asked to confine themselves as much as possible to the practical issue of how the Dutch art world should deal with non-western art.

The debate published here focused on the knowledge gap that yawns between non-western art and critics. Non-western art has been shown for years in Dutch ethnological museums like Amsterdam's Royal Institute for the Tropics and Rotterdam's World Arts Museum. These exhibitions receive scant attention, or none at all, from Dutch art critics, and even when they do make the papers, it is rarely in the arts section. Now that the same work made by the same artists is being exhibited in museums of modern art and biennials, critics complain that they are not competent to judge it because they are unfamiliar with the context. The question triggering this debate was why critics do not regard that context as their business.

The speakers were Janneke Wesseling, Charlotte Huygens and Kitty Zijlmans. Wesseling, art critic on *NRC Handelsblad*, describes her difficulties in judging art from unfamiliar regions. Charlotte Huygens, curator for the Islamic cultural region at the World Arts Museum, focuses on the problem of the reception of non-western art in today's (western dominated) art world. Kitty Zijlmans, professor of recent art history and theory at Leiden University, advocates a broader and more diversified academic art-historical curriculum. Els van der Plas' text for her presentation during the first debate on non-western art, held in Zaal de Unie, follows as an addendum to the debate. Van der Plas, director of the Prince Claus Fund, highlights the aims and context of the policy plan she authored for an unrealized world museum in Almere, the Netherlands.

The debates were titled *The Boundaries of World Art* #1 and #2. The first was organized in association with the Rotterdam Art Foundation in Zaal de Unie on June 22, 2001. It was chaired by Ineke Schwartz. A screening of *De zwarte markt* (the black market), a documentary by Jos van den Bergh on non-western art with interviews of Oladélé Ajiboyé Bamgboyé, Okwui Enwezor and Meschac Gaba, preceded the debate.
The second debate was held at Witte de With on December 6 that same year. The debate coincided with a series of exhibitions of non-western art in Rotterdam. The World Arts Museum showed work by twelve Arab artists, the Boijmans Van Beuningen Museum was preparing for the opening of *Unpacking Europe*, the first Dutch blockbuster show of non-western art. TENT., center for contemporary art, staged an exhibition of Caribbean art, *ARTE di nos e ta*, guest-curated by Adi Martis, a participant in debate #1. The Dutch newspaper *NRC Handelsblad* published Janneke Wesseling's presentation, which prompted a barrage of letters to the editor, including one by co-speaker Charlotte Huygens.

Janneke Wesseling

The Illusion of a Good Conscience

Ali Omar Ermes has painted large, colorful, Arabic characters on sheets of paper. Sturdy wooden struts are fixed to the top and bottom. Ermes is quoting here from *Ode 6* by the poet Antarah ibn Shaddad, the title-card says. I can't read the characters. I am not acquainted with either Ermes or ibn Shaddad. I cannot judge whether the paintings are successful in terms of calligraphy. I do not even know whether these gouaches are meant to relate to the calligraphic tradition. Actually, I haven't the slightest idea what they *do* relate to. Nor do I know what purpose the much too sturdy struts serve: is their function purely esthetic, or do they perhaps refer to an Arabic tradition of mounting paper?

The same goes for the other works in the show *Recent Work by 12 Arab Artists* in the World Arts Museum in Rotterdam. I simply don't know what to make of them. Khairat Al-Saleh makes kitschy porcelain decorated with gold-leaf and lapis lazuli, and etchings on "The Dance of the Arabesque." Mohammed Bennani's etchings look as if they are the work of a latter-day Tapiès epigone, but I haven't the faintest idea where it comes from or whether Bennani is referring to Western art. The only works I can understand are Laila Shawa's lithos. Her work has a political character rendered in an attractive Warhol-like vein. One work is a collage, *Walls of Gaza,* incorporating a dark gateway, the *Passage to Freedom,* her litho *Blood Money* shows a grid of red dollars. In a way, Shawa's work recalls Klaus Staeck's sociopolitical protest prints. A text panel tells us that she is a Palestinian who has been living and working in London for many years.

The work of these Arab artists was selected by the Egee Art Gallery in London, a gallery or dealer I had never heard of before. A brief gloss informs us that the twelve Arab artists are among the best in the world, but fails to enlighten the beholder about their work. Why is this presentation staged in the World Arts Museum and not in a museum of art? Is it perhaps an anthropological exhibition? Where do these people come from, what is their work *about?* What is meant by "the best in the world"? The blurb is probably referring to the best Arab art, for it is obvious that these artists, with the exception of Shawa, have anything but Western art in mind.

To be quite frank, I do not think that this art is good. My opinion is based on intuition, on my visual experience, on what I have seen here and there in the Netherlands and on a few trips to the Middle East, and yes, I do of course apply my own – Western – criteria of art.

But no esthetic questions are asked when we are dealing with non-western art. Nor are any questions asked about its intrinsic quality. The general consensus is that it is by definition right and important for this "other" art to be seen here, for us to provide generous space for it and approach it with an open mind. After all, any criticism would smack of smug Western hegemonic ideas.

In the recent history of (Western) art there is a break somewhere near the end of the sixties. Prior to that, it was taken more or less for granted that the strongest culture was superior to the weaker. Artists appreciated objects from non-western, "primitive" cultures chiefly for their outer form and integrated them into modernism – from Gauguin and Picasso to the *informel* painting of the École de Paris. Nowadays, though, we have the postmodern model: other cultures will assimilate along with our Western democratic values and will promote a worldwide exchange on equal terms. Recently this fairy-tale came to an abrupt end. Meanwhile, the West carries on with its harsh domination of other cultures, a domination that has lasted for centuries and is well on the way to becoming total.

The multicultural illusion is supposed to salve the West's guilty conscience. Globalization in art is the illusory triumph of a decentralized world, a world without frontiers, in which artists can participate in a multicultural dialogue. For the time being, this illusion is being upheld by the international art biennials organized by the West all over the world.

In our immigration country, politics play an important part in supporting this development. Museums and art institutions are rewarded with generous subsidies for drawing attention to "New Netherlanders." This accounts for the flurry of exhibitions focusing on this group since Rick van der Ploeg was appointed Secretary for Culture. The show in the World Arts Museum is only one example from a wide range of events, in cities and towns ranging from the metropolitan agglomeration known as the Ring City to the farthest outposts in the provinces. Money is an important driving force. And in addition to money, the majority of these exhibitions are much concerned with political correctness and not very much with art.

We have only just been liberated from the obligatory appearance of a sole woman in art exhibitions in the degrading capacity of a token female. The role of token nigger or alibi-Ali is of course equally degrading, but that doesn't bother culture officials and exhibition makers. Take the Chinese artist Tiong Ang, born in Surabaya in 1961, a resident of the Netherlands almost all his life and brought up by his parents to speak Dutch. Grinning broadly, he recently told me: "I shout 'pisang ambon' [a banana drink], and get a round of applause."

And so in emulation of World Music we now have World Art. World art is made by people who live in or come from non-western regions. In other words, the term world art sweeps all non-western forms of artistic expression onto one heap. There is however a world of difference between an artist who lives in the West and addresses our art tradition, and an artist whose work is flown here from some African hinterland to an exhibition of world art. What the works have to offer, the stratified nature of art and its inherently ambiguous and transcendental character, are not what count here. The focus is entirely on the higher aim served by the artist and on the political struggle he or she can be identified with.

An example of artists from non-western regions is the celebrated video artist Shirin Neshat. She was born in 1957 in Iran, studied at the University of California at Berkeley from 1974, lives in New York and paid her first return visit to Iran in 1990. Nevertheless, she is invited to all the international exhibitions as a (female) representative of Arab, or Persian, art. Neshat plays this role with enthusiasm, producing modish, nostalgic, quasi-anthropological – in a word: insufferable – films about the clouded relations between Muslim women and their husbands, who are estranged from themselves by Western colonization.

Examples of genuinely original non-western artists are also to be seen in any major exhibition. Take the African Sunday Jack Akpan (1940), whose life-size concrete statues of dead people are based on photographs. These folkloric sculptures have nothing in common with contemporary western art except for the fact that they conform to a myth of originality and a kind of naive primitivism. Akpan is conscious of his role by now: "Natural Authentic Sculptor," it says on his visiting cards.

But, very rarely, an exhibition does succeed in initiating a meaningful dialogue – a dialogue in which the public can participate – between envoys from different cultures. Last month the Center for Visual Arts in Leiden presented the results of a joint project by six refugee artists and six artists from Leiden on the question "What is world art?" Jan Kleingeld's contribution was a number of "peepshows": boxes hung on the wall at eye-level in which he had placed the texts of brief mutual interviews (one interview per box) between two Dutch artists, one from the Sudan and one from Georgia. You look through a hole and see, in the middle of the text, the reflection of your own eye. The text, in mirror-image, is glued to the inside of the front of the box so that its reflection can be read around the reflected eye: an effective image for mutual voyeurism: people observing one another and reflecting one another. The space of the little box coincides exactly with that of the viewer. The texts are in the uncorrected broken English in which the artists conversed – none of them was speaking his/her own language. They are brief summaries of the participants' respective lives, telling us how different Georgia smells – the soil, the water, the market – since communism was replaced by democracy, how Mustafa longs for his wife who is still in the Sudan and has no telephone, about Father Christmas and a song rendered by two popular Dutch cabaret artists. A lovely work, Kleingeld's little boxes, and the only one to address the problem of observing the Other.

It is high time to ask *what* we want to exchange, and why. There is absolutely no sense in creating a mash of world art without doing justice to an artwork's unique, individual character. Just as there is no sense in engaging in dialogue with other cultures if we no longer attach any importance to our own cultural values and barely know what our own culture stands for. We are ignoring a fact that is inherent in a culture, perhaps its most important characteristic: the desire to conquer another culture. As Webster's Unabridged Dictionary puts it so nicely, culture is "the act of developing by education, discipline, social experience: the training or refining of the moral and intellectual faculties."

I would very much like to become acquainted with contemporary art from other cultures. Pasolini once described art in a general sense as "enjoying in freedom someone else's freedom," an excellent definition which moreover seems to be gaining relevance more and more. I look forward to art institutes, exhibition makers and subsidizers giving us an opportunity to really encounter those other cultures, by taking art seriously, by making insightful, well-considered exhibitions – in short, to treat art, its makers and its viewers with dignity.

Charlotte Huygens

Art from the Islamic World in Dutch Cultural Institutions

Islamic Art in the European World

Art from the Islamic world is a wide-ranging term, embracing an artistic production of at least fourteen centuries, from countries in which Islam is or has been an important cultural factor. It stands for religious and secular art-forms, applied and autonomous art, whether inspired by the Islamic heritage or not, for creations conforming to some of these criteria or embodying a combination of them.

Be that as it may, Islamic art is not exclusively non-western art; it goes back a long way in the European field of culture. Islamic art is undeniably an integral part of a variety of European artistic traditions ranging from the architecture of Andalusia and Sicily to Berlage's Municipal Museum at The Hague, from masterpieces of literature by Dante and Goethe to the poems of Leopold, from paintings by Giotto and later Renaissance painters and also orientalistic painters up to Escher. Dutch majolica, Venetian glass, most of the instruments in western orchestras: all these examples, due to their provenance or their source of inspiration, have direct links with the Middle East. In terms of cultural history there is every justification for Islamic art in the Louvre and the British Museum, places comparable with the heritage of "our" classics. Even so, you can graduate as an art historian in the Netherlands without ever having actually studied Islamic art.

Although I am all for a dynamic definition of art and culture unbounded by static ethnic borders or by a western classification into high and low arts, I do believe that the country of provenance (in the sense of a cultural cradle) of works of art and their makers is an important factor. Cultural backgrounds are relevant, also in the case of artists based in the Netherlands or Europe whose links with – in this case – the Islamic cultural region are confined to their childhood. Visual development from infancy as well as, say, a bilingual upbringing are crucial for a person's general development, as scientific research continues to demonstrate with growing conviction. These factors influence creative processes too. John Onians, guest professor in the progressive department of "art history from a worldwide perspective" at Leiden University, can tell you all about it. Children's drawings supply even more fascinating evidence to support that proposition. And while people are constantly trying to create a meaningful past for themselves, a foreign background can retain its significance for generation after generation.

Although it is the privilege of contemporary artists to indicate the context or contexts, the cultural perspectives, in which they want their work to be seen, this does not mean that artists are always the best exegetes of their own work.

Ethnological Museums and Art Museums, Galleries

In the Netherlands, non-western art was traditionally the domain of the ethnological museums. Museums of art confined – and confine – themselves chiefly to western art. This regional boundary has been crossed in recent years: we have seen art from Surinam in the Stedelijk Museum, *Pavillon du Maroc* in the Boijmans Van Beuningen Museum, African art in the Beelden aan Zee Museum. Conversely, Rotterdam's Museum of Ethnology, renamed World Arts Museum [Wereldmuseum], devotes structural attention to the relationship between other cultures and the Netherlands. From a demographic point of view it is no coincidence that this change into a World Arts Museum was prompted by the museum for children it incorporates, known as Travel Palace [Het Reispaleis]. It must be said that incorporating non-western art in museums other than ethnological museums is rarely structural policy at present, and this is a pity for several reasons.

We are not seeing enough attempts to make use of the specific expertise of ethnological museums. For example, the Boijmans Van Beuningen Museum chose work by Rachid Koraichi for its exhibition *Unpacking Europe* without informing the World Arts Museum – in spite of the fact that his work has not only been on show in two of the World Arts Museum's earlier exhibitions, but is also represented in its permanent collection. In my opinion the borderlines between museum presentations and collections ought not to be so rigid; in accordance with scholarly insights and social developments they should be constantly questioned, and attuned to one another. The aforementioned work by Koraichi was selected in the World Arts Museum in accordance with criteria from Arab art history and as such in line with the museum's historical collection. It is a point of departure quite unlike that of *Unpacking Europe,* whose guest-curators focused on the relationship with Europe. This difference in approach results in interesting extra dimensions, for Arab criteria can differ strongly from western ones, witness the contrast between Janneke Wesseling's negative reaction to works in our exhibition and the fact that the participating artists are stars in the Arab-Islamic world, where their work is greatly admired. One does however wonder how an art historian who has visited the Middle East managed to overlook the most important school of modernism, to which Ali Omar Ermes, cited by Wesseling, belongs.

The art related to the Islamic world on show in Dutch galleries is a very mixed bag in terms of quality, but I do admire the galleries' initiative and the concomitant commercial risk they are prepared to take.

The Place of Islamic Art in a Western Canon

How, then, can art from the Islamic world be placed and/or judged within the canon of western art? I confine myself to contemporary visual art here, which on the world's stage must defend itself as a minority against a world of art dominated by western values. In many Islamic countries the art academies are already a hundred years old. They are modeled on western examples and tuition conforms to western standards. There are moreover museums, collectors, biennials, art markets and incipient art criticism. Being an artist in the Arab world, implies that one belongs to a very small elite, which is why I think that a phenomenon as necessary as art criticism is less strongly developed in the Arab world. We are talking here about a small in-crowd in which everybody knows everybody else. Nevertheless, art from this field claims to be universal and may certainly be assessed in an exclusively western context. Some artists prefer this. But meanwhile art has undergone autonomous developments in search of a post-colonial identity of its own. Broadly speaking, this has resulted in two schools: art which in the widest sense conforms to Islamic tradition and is clearly inspired by Arab characters, and art which resorts to a national artistic vocabulary: Berber culture in Morocco, the Pharaonic heritage in Egypt, Byzantine traditions in Syria, et cetera. An exclusively western viewpoint can therefore be constrictive. In terms of philosophical esthetics it is desirable to interpret artistic creations in the utmost detail before passing judgment. Comparisons must be made with work by other artists in the same school, a relationship must be established with local cultural history and the public's frame of reference. Ethnological museums are ideally equipped for this task. Whether in an ethnological context or not, however, judgment – even of the most hybrid art – must be supported by a wide range of well-considered arguments, and unfortunately this does not always happen.

I wish to examine briefly – and must therefore of necessity generalize on – three fundamental criteria for quality in art: proficiency, the power of expression, and originality.

Proficiency is traditionally linked in the Islamic world with technical expertise and craftsmanship – against the background of the religious esthetic of Islam: the idea that God makes himself known in the glory of creation. You are probably reminded of Plato, and rightly so, but unlike Plato's theory, art in this interpretation, in keeping with its nature, is not an inferior representation of a higher reality but a reflection of God. God's characteristics can be classified under beauty and majesty. A remarkable parallel with Kant's perception of the beautiful and the sublime comes to mind. In the Islamic perception the two concepts are closely linked, and that is expressed in art. Not just directly, in a predilection for motifs derived from nature and sublimated abstraction, but also, and hence all the more urgently, in abhorrence of what Janneke Wesseling in her review of the exhibition *Jetztzeit* describes as "deliberate, but uncalled-for ugliness." The Islamic world still upholds esthetic standards such as visual harmony, symmetry, and ideal proportion (drawn from calligraphy as the supreme art-form) and, stemming from the religious prohibition of idolatry, a strong tendency towards stylization and symbolic representation as opposed to realism. Whereas in the West the transition to the modern age was characterized by increasing abstraction, things are the other way round in the Islamic world.

Seen through western eyes, traditionally oriented eastern art tends to be superficially described as "too decorative." You may thus dismiss eastern preferences as unfathomable, but in the western esthetic too there are movements which yield subtler points of reference. The structuralist school concentrates on formal criteria which can provide surprising new insights. Against the background described above, sculptor Faisal Samra states: "I would like to apologize to the viewer who is looking in my work for ornamental beauty. I am a lover of the beauty of the soul, which I strive to achieve through austere and unadorned material."

The power of expression is closely associated with language and the ability (through language) to comprehend a concept. Cornel Bierens, and in this he is certainly not alone, argued in the newspaper *NRC Handelsblad* of October 15, 1999, that art in our time has turned entirely into concept, and hence language and explanation. A matter of great significance for anyone desirous of understanding art from another culture. It is no coincidence that all reviews of our exhibition *Recent Work by Twelve Arab Artists* showered praise on the work of Palestinian artist Laila Shawa, who epitomizes a western public's expectations of what the Middle East has to offer. In the Palestinian Diaspora and in dictatorships, art is the perfect sanctuary and also the perfect answer to social injustice. Due to its many hidden messages however, this political art is often hard to fathom. The work of, say, Farid Belkahia, one of Morocco's celebrated painters, is hardly ever presented as engaged, political art, because people emphasize the Berber elements not as political but as folkloric elements from Morocco. Nevertheless, this work is really political. In an exhibition by Chris Dercon not so long ago in the Kunsthal it was said, on the basis of conversations with the artists themselves, that the work of young artists in the West isn't about anything at all. Belkahia's work *is* about something, though; it stands for an ideal.

Originality seems to be a self-evident criterion, although not without reason does a recent book about beauty in Arab culture dwell on the question of whether there is any originality at all in the arts. This has long been doubted in Western sources. Of course the question should be answered in the affirmative, but it does indicate a huge difference of opinion. Let me cite an example: the famous Egyptian singer Umm Kulthum could fill an evening with new musical variants of just one poem written long ago. The audience had not come for the new songs but for the originality of her vocal re-interpretations and the continuing search for perfection.

The Critic

A last word about the role of the critic. In the best of all possible situations the critic, as an expert, is the intermediary between exhibition, curator and artist on the one hand and the general public on the other. Where works should speak for themselves in the gallery, where extra links might be forged or horizons explored, the critic can make his or her knowledge available and give the interested visitor, listener or reader something to go by. A good critic meets the public's expectations, and that public has changed a lot over the past twenty-five years. Of course a critic may pass judgment, but carefully and (in this role) in compliance with the proper journalistic principles of letting both sides have their say. Today's art – and certainly the hybrid, transcultural art-forms which are the focus of this evening – needs, by its very nature, new theories. Essential for this is open debate, with respect for cultural differences but without prejudices and predetermined results.

Kitty Zijlmans

Looking at Art from a Global Perspective: a Reconsideration of Esthetic Judgement

Western art historians have a problem with what the German historian Thomas Nipperdey defined so nicely as "blinded by nearness" ("durch Nahsicht verblendet"): focusing on something so closely that you don't see the rest. It's time for us to look further than our western boundaries and seriously study and evaluate the art and material culture of other regions. Actually, it's fascinating to see art developing worldwide and getting to know it. According to art critic Thomas McEvilly it is not only fascinating but necessary if we don't want to miss the boat somewhere along the way: "If we don't more fully engage the contemporary art of Asia, Africa, and Latin America, we may wake up one day to find that the art history of our time was happening elsewhere and we failed to notice it."[1] The world is changing, art is changing and, *mutatis mutandis,* so is art history. This does not happen of its own accord; art history needs rewriting and art historians have to do it. Not only must we take a fresh look at what is happening in art but, equally important if not even more so, we have to take a critical look at our premises and points of departure: how was art history written thus far, what are its points of departure and on what conception of art is it based, what art have we excluded and what were our reasons for doing so? None of this is happening in art criticism, nor in museums or in art history.

I think that Dutch art critics and historians ought to show their colors more often. By that I mean that they should indicate the frame of reference in which they operate and what conception of art is implicitly anchored in it. We take our western concept of art so much for granted that we apparently feel no urge to make it manifest, because it is the norm, the dominant discourse, and therefore remains invisible. Nonetheless, it is the benchmark. Displaying one's own point of departure creates space for dialogue and exchange with other perspectives. Awareness of one's own subjective viewpoint and one's own points of departure are essential for a discriminating judgment.

1. Thomas McEvilly, "Tracking the Indian Diaspora," *Art in America,* vol. 86, no. 1 (October 1998): 79.

Museums, too, are confused by the fact that the dominant discourse remains invisible. Museums of art display "our" art, ethnological museums the rest of the world's artefacts. This is not a neutral classification; it is highly colored and hierarchical. Western scholarship studies "the other," charts it and exhibits its artefacts and customs in an ethnological museum. That is not how we treat ourselves; western civilization is *a priori* our point of departure. Our artworks hang and stand in *special* museums. These art temples place the artwork by definition in an esthetic context which is acknowledged by us all and rarely disputed. We do occasionally squabble about what is displayed in those museums, but frayed tempers are soon soothed. Jeff Koons' "pig" has long since been accepted. Art in museum collections (i.e. leading museums, for the art world is strictly hierarchical) is indicative for the process of canonization and historiography. We are talking about only a tiny percentage here, a group of artworks selected on the basis of prevailing but seldom explicitly stated esthetic standards. Quality is the yardstick; isn't it striking how closely the collections in modern art museums resemble one another? There's no such thing as *one* quality, though. Quality is dependent on a system of norms and values. Quality is assigned. That is the problem with art from other regions. What system of values is applied? The modern western art temple's system of values. That is why we see so much of a the same there, and so little – if any – art from other cultures.

A considerable amount of art is being produced in non-European regions, as we have seen over the past few years, and it calls for attention and evaluation. Where should that be done? Where should the works be housed? Ethnological museums, being based on anthropological points of departure and issues, have never evinced a special interest in works of art. For a long time these museums presented a rather static picture of other cultures. However, now that they want to forge closer links with current developments, contemporary art has become relevant and they are wondering what to call themselves. Rotterdam opted for a World Arts Museum in which, although multicultural Rotterdam is on show, there is still no place for indigenous, western cultures. That might offend historical and suchlike museums. Nevertheless, contemporary art – but not western – is now exhibited in (and sometimes collected by) ethnological museums. The context this creates for that art is linked with the tradition of its country of origin. That is one possibility, but it has its snags. After all, the context of an ethnological museum is quite different from that of an art museum, and art museums have high thresholds which are built on western standards.

We really do have to reconsider our premises with regard to quality in art, our normative perception of there being only one standard, and our categorical arrangements (see the museums). A change of mentality of this kind will be an arduous process, and there we have a task for the media, museums and art history.

To me, art history is a field which studies the rich diversity of a society as expressed in products of past and present material and visual culture. The limits of that field are not fixed but flexible, and should, on the basis of new theories and insights generated by a society's cultural dynamics, be constantly re-examined. Currently, those dynamics are all about processes of globalization, and art history has to react to these processes. It is a long time since art history confined itself to studying the "masterpieces" of an elite culture. Instead, it aims at revealing the cultural and artistic reciprocities and interactions between the various social domains.

We have access to the whole world and are increasingly confronted by the art and culture of societies other than our own. That is the consequence of ongoing developments in art worldwide, the presence of migrant artists, and Holland's changing demography. Art history cannot ignore these factors. That is why the department of art history at Leiden University has opted for a new orientation and decided to study the history of art from a global perspective. Leiden is a more likely choice than other Dutch universities, for its department of art history is part of the humanities faculty, where languages and cultures from all over the world are studied. The prime consideration, though, is that in 2001 art history can no longer ignore art produced – in both the present and the past – by the rest of the world. Learning about art from other regions – and this is perfectly feasible, for there is plenty of material, and translations of relevant texts are available – can also change our perception of our own art and compel us to be more explicit about our frames of reference.

For the study of art history at Leiden, the global perspective means that from their first year, students have three lines of approach to the visual art and material culture from regions other than the west. In the first place they are introduced to the art and material culture of non-western civilizations by colleagues from those fields. The second approach focuses on interactions, mutual influences and interculturalization processes in art and culture. And the third addresses methodical-theoretical reflection on art history in a global perspective. The aim here is to formulate a theoretical framework for the study of art worldwide, thereby arriving at, for want of a better term, "comparative art history." This is not a single, clear-cut approach but a wide area of research focused on a more integral, comparative study of art and material culture worldwide. All kinds of interesting approaches are conceivable. Investigation of the concepts that inform our perspective on art can pinpoint universalistic or relativistic points of departure. Research into the representation of "the other" in art and material products is both fascinating and revealing. In what way do notions of nationalism, identity and ethnicity play a part in the historiography of (western) art? What insights are to be gained by seeing the art history of other cultures in relation to our own?

Searching for relationships and analogies with other cultural regions makes sense, because cultures are not separate entities but have things in common, and in certain aspects may be compared with one another. Cultures are changing all the time; they are dynamic and heterogeneous. Although cultural borders can be observed, they have to be redefined for each period. This also means that we may not proceed from a fixed center and its hierarchically inferior periphery (i.e. the West and the rest of the world), but from a flexible model of centers and peripheries. Karel van Kooij, specialized in Southern Asian art, prefers to speak of a cultural wave rather than a cultural region.[2] Cultural waves appear and ebb away, but they leave traces, residues (examples are Hellenism or Islamicization). The term "cultural wave" pins nothing down; it takes into account the nonstop process of change that is constantly linking and re-separating regions.

Employing these terms to describe the influence of modern art on the world as a cultural wave which has left its traces but then ebbed away, we can find out what residue was left, what happened to it and, above all, where and how people pushed forward in art and where they reverted to their own traditions. When we understand "modern" as a stance, as turning one's back on tradition, we see a diversity of modernisms in the world, modernisms which cropped up in different regions at different times and steered their

2. K.R. van Kooij, *Lichaam in Beeld. Kunst van India in iconologisch en vergelijkend perspectief* (inaugural speech as professor of the Art History of Southern Asia at the University of Leiden, March 1, 1996).

own courses. That is the frame of reference for the works of art; it does not reduce them to western derivatives. It might also help art criticism and art history to shed their blinkers. It is strange to see how strongly modern art and the modern perception of art have wielded their influence to this day. When all's said and done, we are talking here about a perception of art that was not current in Western Europe prior to Kant and which the esthetic formalism of Greenbergian modernism has put to flight. This excluded so much art – western art too – that one might ask whether *l'art pour l'art* was the exception rather than the rule in the art world, even though today's opinion of art is formed along the same lines to a large extent. The norm of the modern art temple still stakes its universal claims, although its esthetic judgment is restricted and highly specific. It certainly is dominant, at any rate here in Western Europe. Studies like John Clark's *Modern Asian Art*,[3] and journals like *Third Text* and *Art Asia Pacific* have long been putting the hegemony of the West into perspective, renounced western-influenced ideology some time ago, and employ pluriform frames of reference: those of dialogue, of discursiveness. It is time for us to follow suit, otherwise indeed one day we might find out that the art history of our time was happening somewhere else and we hadn't even noticed.

3. John Clark, *Modern Asian Art* (Sydney: 1998).

Charlotte Huygens, Janneke Wesseling and Kitty Zijlmans

Debate

Valentijn Byvanck

I have a question about the market. Everybody is talking about what on the one hand we refer to as our changing society, a broadening of the canon, but what we really mean is how the Dutch market is changing and how people are getting interested in other matters. My first question is for Janneke Wesseling: however much I agree with you on the great importance of respecting the values anchored in the canon, you must surely acknowledge the surge of all kinds of other values and ideas that is taking place, to which you as a reviewer ought to react simply because readers want to know about those new things.

Janneke Wesseling

I haven't the slightest objection to that. I mean it when I say I'd like very much to be cognizant of these matters. As Kitty Zijlmans has already said, we can't understand anything without a frame of reference. And when I was talking about that exhibition at the beginning of my lecture, I wasn't reviewing it. Never in my life have I dealt with twelve artists in twenty lines. I was merely describing the dilemma in which I find myself in an exhibition without any frame of reference. I repeat, it's wonderful that those things can be shown here and I take it for granted that they are often enriching. But the interesting fact is that all the questions this raises no longer matter when you're confronted with a really good artist, oeuvre or work. Nam June Paik is an example, as are Yayoi Kusama and Meschac Gaba. Kusama comes from a Japanese tradition, Nam June Paik from Korea, and Meschac Gaba is from Benin. And yet they are able to convey meaning; their work has such a universal eloquence that these questions are no longer relevant. What does it matter that Kusama comes from Japan?

Kitty Zijlmans

They wouldn't agree with you there. I had Paik in mind in the context of oriental studies, which are slowly coming our way. These studies accuse western art history of having appropriated Nam June Paik and failing to acknowledge his roots, his Korean and Buddhist background.

Janneke Wesseling

I don't see why. The Buddhist background of his work is perfectly obvious to me. Another example is Lee Ufan, who is a Buddhist painter. It's very interesting to see his work; it bears a resemblance to our Minimal Art, and yet you feel and understand that it comes from a different tradition.

Kitty Zijlmans

But your frame of reference is Minimal Art.

Janneke Wesseling

That's right.

Charlotte Huygens

Apart from that, I think the context in which you approach art matters a lot. Rachid Koraichi's work is now on view in Museum Boijmans Van Beuningen. Before that, it was in the British Museum, where there was not the slightest doubt as to its quality, but as soon as it comes to the World Arts Museum in Rotterdam, people start asking questions. I see the same thing happening with Ali Omar Ermes. His work is highly esteemed all over the world – with the exception, I might almost say, of Europe and the United States. The term "universal" is closely linked with western art criteria. When people say an artist has made an international breakthrough, they mean a breakthrough in Europe or the United States, not that it has broken through from the Middle East to China, Japan, Malaysia or Indonesia.

Audience

How come this quality is not questioned in the British Museum, but it is in the Netherlands?

Charlotte Huygens

I think it has something to do with the fact that the artists in question are very keen to be presented in the western tradition. In their opinion the work should speak for itself. That is why, at the artists' explicit request, we captioned their work with texts which they themselves submitted. The one is lengthier than the other, but they're all very brief. As curator, I would rather have assigned much more importance to the cultural context. Visitors to an ethnological museum expect it. Without that background they have only their western art-historical background to go by. I think a reviewer ought to acquire that knowledge. If the information you need is not provided, all you have to do is pick up the phone. Surveys have shown that the average visitor is pretty good at finding information, but a reviewer comes with a specialist training and sees things from another angle.

Audience

Does it matter that these artists want to be seen without a context? Isn't that what western artists want as well?

Charlotte Huygens

They overlook the fact that the visitor interprets their work from a western context. Because they exhibit a lot in their own context – the Arab world or, if they are exiles, in Paris where there is a bigger market and much more knowledge of Islamic culture than here – they are used to people looking at their work quite differently. Arab artists aren't aware of Holland's special position, in Europe too. In Holland there are no galleries specializing in Islamic art, no dealers or museums for it, and very few collections. Even if you tell artists this, they still want to be presented out of their context. They want to be seen and appreciated according to western standards. And of course we fully respect that wish, although I do think a lot is lost because of it. I understand the opposition of the Dutch-based Arab artist Laila Meliani to the kind of exoticism conjured up by her being a Moroccan artist. But I do want to emphasize that presenting art in an Arabic historical context is just as serious as in a western historical context. Art institutions are depriving themselves by not making use of the opportunity to present the different perspectives of the work. I also maintain that Rachid Koraichi's work could be shown simultaneously in an ethnological and an art museum. You'd see the work from two completely different angles.

Audience

Does the esthetic aspect still play a part in selecting artists?

Charlotte Huygens

Janneke Wesseling asserts that esthetic issues are not addressed. That is not true; esthetic issues and the criterion of quality were paramount in the selection for this show.

Janneke Wesseling

You didn't understand me properly. I am talking about non-western art presented in a western context. I am talking about the whole of that broad sweep of biennials and the way non-western art is received here and organized by curators. From the discourse on that subject you grasp that as soon as non-western art crops up, it is no longer *bon ton* to ask esthetic questions.

Audience

A lot of art-theoretical concepts proceed from the idea of homogeneity; *the* art of the west, *the* culture of Europe – they are presented as entities. Anything else is automatically non-western, non-European culture. I think this is a very simplistic view. People forget that European culture is similarly divided. My question is: what is art like beyond that division?

Kitty Zijlmans

Well, I don't think the terminology should be changed, but it certainly ought to be adapted or expanded. What I always point out from the very beginning is my explicit stance: where do I stand, where am I coming from, what is my approach? That is a perspective and it also defines a limit, for I can't look at things differently from the way I learned to look and how I've been trained to look. But I *can* define that way of looking and then see whether it might be a feasible method for examining certain forms or manifestations. And I also look at what is going on in anthropology, sociology or literature, what systems of concepts are employed. But these are of course all constructions for describing something. It is very difficult to be more explicit and to deploy that explicit definition of one's own concept of art as an instrumentarium and say: this is the part I play in looking at something, this is how I as a subject look at that object, that's the extent of my perspective. Different perspectives need not be mutually exclusive and who knows, maybe dialogue can widen the scope.

Charlotte Huygens

My background is naturally always part of my baggage. That's why it is so important in an exhibition of Arab art, that local art critics make catalogues and write reviews from their own cultural perspective. That's where our museum has an advantage over a museum like Boijmans. I'd like to add that this kind of problem is encountered chiefly with contemporary art, which is dominated so strongly by the west: the dominant political factor of the moment. In mediaeval Arab art the dominant factor was China, and so it is quite wrong to say that art was more authentic before then. It was oriented towards another region. The fact that the dominant factor is now our western world has a strong effect on the debate, because not only artists but also curators, gallery-owners and reviewers are presumed to grasp everything immediately, something they were not expected to do in old art.

Kitty Zijlmans

What particularly strikes me about your reply is that in your museum, context – and I wonder what that means exactly – is created by reviews and catalogues by indigenous people from the region; Boijmans does not create such a context. I am inclined to say, it does not need to, because it is an art museum where different standards apply and where apparently there is less of a need to explain culture and establish a context. This illustrates so very clearly how our museums are separate domains. As long as artists are associated with an ethnological museum, I don't think they'll ever get away from it.

Valentijn Byvanck

Isn't it rather strange? Here we have three speakers in search of a context, but the artists don't want it, and neither, really, do the art institutes.

Charlotte Huygens

What we are actually seeing at present is that art museums are doing more and more about contextualization. The Hieronymus Bosch exhibition is one example; another was the Brancusi show at the Centre Pompidou a few years ago. They were brimming with context, whereas presentations in ethnological museums are gradually abandoning context. They do offer a lot of information, but they do it somewhere else, for example via the computer or in the library.

Valentijn Byvanck

But presenting Bosch in his own period is an essentially different type of context. You can hardly imagine discussing contemporary art in the same way as you tell the World Arts Museum's visitors how they are supposed to look at Arab art?

Janneke Wesseling

Shouldn't we try to see this from the artist's perspective? All the artists I know are highly conscious of the context they work in. This is confirmed by exhibition practice, by the kind of exhibitions they make, by their chosen venue. They also realize perfectly well that context is an important factor in the way their work is regarded. Indeed, a western artist is censured for failing to account for the context of a place he uses. I think that's a good thing, because art is governed by context. Conversely, when an Arab artist comes to Holland to exhibit his work, he evidently wants to be viewed in that western context. That's what I also sense in what Charlotte Huygens was saying. He wants to relate to it. So what's wrong about my trying to see him in that context? There's no way I could possibly see him from an Arab perspective.

Charlotte Huygens

I sense a kind of ambivalence on the part of the artists. If they present their work in our museum under the heading of Arab art, to which a standard of quality may be assigned, then it is in the context of our museum and that means that we show it in the light of Arab art history. If those artists want to be judged by western standards, and they all say they do, then Museum Boijmans Van Beuningen is the place for them. But they would not be presenting themselves as Arab artists there, and sometimes it can all fall flat. And then I agree with many of Wesseling's reviews, like the one on *Documenta X* in Kassel, or *Continental Shift* at Maastricht. You have to make a choice and then judge the work according to the criteria implied by that choice. If you judge an exhibition in our museum by western art-historical standards and come to the conclusion that the exhibition has its shortcomings, I have to argue that such is absolutely not the case with Arab art-historical standards, as is confirmed by the prestigious prizes awarded to these artists whose work can be seen in Arab museums all over the world. Not because of the folkloric elements, I observe that some museums of art history think it is interesting to present aboriginal art, but chiefly dot-paintings or Rachid Koraichi, especially the work inspired by talismans.

Valentijn Byvanck

Kitty Zijlmans, do you teach your students to employ an Arab context when they look at contemporary Arab art and with a western context when they look at today's western art? Because what Charlotte Huygens is really suggesting is that these perspectives should be kept separate.

Charlotte Huygens

What I'm suggesting is to look at the work from more perspectives. Look at it in Museum Boijmans, from the perspective Boijmans offers. But also show it in the World Arts Museum, which possesses the knowledge that will enable you to comprehend other elements in it, to see it in a longer tradition.

Valentijn Byvanck

So Kitty Zijlmans' students would have to learn different vocabularies – one for the art museum, the other for the ethnological museum.

Kitty Zijlmans

Essential aspects that crop up when I discuss these things with my students are: where did you see something, how was that choice made, how is it hung in the gallery – those are the questions to be asked. It also depends on the viewing level you choose: you can go to a museum and simply enjoy what you see. You can go further – and students of art history owe it to themselves and to their field of study to proceed further – and examine the work more closely. But this is not objective. You use perspectives or an instrumentarium, which can help you, gain access to the work. And then comes the question: this artist is of Arab origin; does that play a role in his work? If so, how? A student of mine will have to learn Persian because he wants to read what is written in the work of a particular artist. He can ask other questions for which he may not need the language. What interests me is the wide choice of possible perspectives for your relationship to art, and I think it's a terrible pity to reduce them to essentialistic questions. It's like saying: an Arab artist, oh, that explains everything. And you won't have learnt a single thing! It is vital to keep on asking how far you can go in assigning meaning to a work.

Audience

I think you're on very dangerous ground there. You're mushing everything up together. An art historian should differentiate, not adopt a subjective attitude to things.

Kitty Zijlmans

And what do you mean by differentiation?

Audience

What nobody has said this evening is that cultures do differ considerably and that so many of those differences remain uncharted. Typical of western art are concepts, ideas, *zeitgeist*, which don't occur in other cultures or only in quite a different way.

Charlotte Huygens

The idea of time and period in art history is very important, but I don't think this has anything to do with the discussion of scholarship's freedom from value-judgments. I think it's a good thing that we no longer think in such absolutist terms these days and say that scholarship is free from value judgments. Establishing formal criteria is always connected with one's own perspective; there comes a time when a person has acquired so much renown as a scholar or critic that his position entitles him to apply those criteria with some authority. I think that is quite legitimate. In my opinion the dilemmas in contemporary art are caused by applying modernistic values like honesty and purity, which have quite different meanings in different contexts. Are non-European artists free to uphold such values, and how can they do so?

Janneke Wesseling

But when we are talking about art, are we not precisely talking about the connection between work and context? Formal connections, content, there is an amalgam of associations that makes a work of art important and meaningful. I don't think I could get through to an Arab, African or other work of art – often they are not works of art at all, but rituals or suchlike – in this way, let alone understand its iconography. For example: I am able to recognize Shiva or Ganesha, and I have an inkling as to what kinds of gods they are, but maybe an artist is not concerned with that kind of thing. Of course he can use them, but it's easy to confuse subject and content. I am unable to understand a work of art from another culture in that way. That is why I disagree with Zijlmans' remark in her introduction that the past is just as alien to us as a different culture [deleted in her revision of the text, ed.]. I do understand the idealism conveyed by that remark and

I even wish it were so, but in my experience and perception it is simply not true. I feel reasonably familiar with the history of the Netherlands and West Europe, and when I visit Florence or Rome I can identify and comprehend much of what I see there.

Kitty Zijlmans

Because you've studied art history.

Janneke Wesseling

And because I am part of my society.

Audience

I want newspapers to select reviewers who tell us about today's art, not someone on the staff who says: I have a western perspective on art. Reviewers have an informative responsibility.

Janneke Wesseling

That's what we've been talking about all the time. I have never reviewed an exhibition of contemporary art in an ethnological museum, because it is not a platform for the discourse to which I relate. That is why it was a good thing that when the newspaper *NRC Handelsblad* decided to carry a review of that exhibition, Sandra Smallenburg conducted interviews, which I consider an appropriate form.[1] An alternative would of course have been to say that only an Arab critic could review the exhibition.

Audience

It doesn't have to be an Arab critic, just someone who gives us information. That's what readers expect. How do you obtain your information? By reading everything?

Janneke Wesseling

Everything I can lay my hands on.

Audience

So why not read about Arab art?

1. Sandra Smallenburg is an art critic writing for *NRC Handelsblad*.

Janneke Wesseling

I wouldn't know where to start.

Charlotte Huygens

Expertise in this field is sparse in Holland. There are museum curators for Dutch pottery from 1600 to 1615, but ethnological museums have to make do with one curator to cover a period of 1500 years in an area of 5000 kilometers.

Janneke Wesseling

This is complicating the issue. We're contradicting each other, because Arab artists *wish* to relate to western art. You yourself said it doesn't matter who exhibits what, as long as the angle of approach is kept clear. That clarity is exactly what is missing.

Charlotte Huygens

In any case now it's in print, it is quite influential. In Wesseling's NRC review she mentions "sturdy struts" whose purpose she could not fathom.[2] But a reviewer can phone the museum and demand information, can't she? After all, the reviewer is the intermediary between an exhibition and the public.

Janneke Wesseling

I didn't write a review of that exhibition.

Charlotte Huygens

Readers can't tell the difference, they read what you wrote and interpret it as a negative review.

Valentijn Byvanck

If readers don't like what they read in the paper, they won't buy it. I know quite a number of NRC readers who grumble about our changing society and are pleased to see their opinion confirmed in some critics' pieces.

2. Wesseling's piece was printed in NRC *Handelsblad* the day after the debate. Charlotte Huygens' reply was printed a week later in the same newspaper.

Charlotte Huygens

That is exactly what immigrant readers, New Netherlanders, deplore: that a large number of participants in the multi-cultural debate haven't the slightest interest in a deeper approach.

Valentijn Byvanck

It's a transitional period. What is new doesn't have to be reflected in everything all the time, does it? It's the friction between different viewpoints that fuels this kind of debate.

Els van der Plas

The Boundaries of World Art

Happily the days are gone when a curator of a major Dutch museum asked me: "*Is* there any modern art in India?" It was 1988, shortly before the exhibition *Les magiciens de la terre* (1989) opened in Paris, the year in which the intercultural journal *Third Text* was just getting off the ground in England and a year before the exhibition *The Other Story* (1989) in London's Hayward Gallery, focusing on African and Asian artists in England, had been slated by the critics. It was the eve of the important *Chinese Modern Art* show at the National Gallery in Beijing (1989), which the authorities closed down the next day, a prelude to the riots on Tiennamen Square. It was the year of Wim Beeren's preparations for *UABC* (1989), an exhibition of Latin-American artists for the Stedelijk Museum. It was the year in which I set up the Gate Foundation in Amsterdam.

In this period Europe and America developed an interest, albeit patchy, in contemporary art from other cultures. These first steps towards a "truly" international contemporary art world prepared the ground for initiatives such as exhibitions with work by contemporary artists from different parts of the world.[1] At the same time these exhibitions and works were a scathing attack on western art history.

The tentative intercultural activities of the eighties are to be seen in a historical perspective reaching much further back than the twentieth century. The difficulty of assessing the value of so-called "non-western" art in those days was a consequence of a centuries-old philosophy that upheld the superiority of European art. Colonialism, slavery and the post-colonial period bear witness to this Eurocentric view with its strictly one-way optimistic concept of progress. It was only as the twentieth century was drawing to a close that these ideas were seriously discussed, in the art world too, but without an appropriate alternative philosophy being offered in their place.

In 1996 two advisors from the Almere town council paid a visit to the Gate Foundation. They were interested in the organization's objectives, which

1. On "true internationalism" see Els van der Plas, "Internationalism and the Arts: Theory and Practice," *Prince Claus Fund Journal*, no. 1 (The Hague: 1998): 55-58.

included the stimulation of intercultural activities in the field of the visual arts, as a basis for a new museum in Almere. According to the assignment, it had to be a museum, and this museum had to differ from other cultural institutions.

Assuming that what Almere wanted was a traditional museum, I wrote in my advisory proposal that a museum in the traditional sense ought to have a collection, a collection unlike any other, whether national or international. Postponing for the moment questions pertaining to the definition, shape, and parameters of the collection, my proposal was to focus on developments in the modern art of Asia, Africa, Latin America and the Caribbean region. This collection should be able to relate to other (museum) collections with a view to forging links, promoting exchanges and conveying information. The museum's program would have to be geared to the definitive points of departure for the collection and the museum as a whole.

By and large, collections of international modern art in the Netherlands and Europe are similar. They all boast examples of early twentieth-century Cubism (Picasso, Braque, Gris), a few French Impressionists and German Expressionists, a De Kooning, North American Minimalists. More recent acquisitions include Nauman, Warhol and a Koons before proceeding to Tracey Emin, Rineke Dijkstra and Stan Douglas. Although they claim to be "international," most museum collections of contemporary art present a one-sided (i.e. western) face. This concept of internationalism is based on the exclusion of everything non-western. In recent years exhibition practice has been changing, becoming more international, but collections lag behind in these developments.

Ethnological museums have endeavored to fill this gap in the "international art-world" by staging exhibitions and in some cases forming small collections from an anthropological angle, without resorting to art-historical expertise. They thus make a valuable contribution to the art world in terms of knowledge and images. Yet, contemporary art, wherever it comes from, ought to be shown in modern art museums, particularly when such museums present themselves as international.

The universal benefit to be gained from assembling any collection whatsoever is the creation of national and international memory. In other words, with a collection you write history, in this case the history of art. The fact that Europe's colonial history is virtually ignored in the formation of modern art collections is a cause for concern. France has founded academies of art in Senegal and Mali. England has done so in Zimbabwe and India, the Netherlands in Indonesia, and Portugal in Angola and Mozambique, to name but a few. Western history has thus become a worldwide issue. In the West, though, this colonial part of the history of European art is missing. Creating a collection based on modern art from these decolonized countries could fill that historical gap.

The so-called non-western part of the world covers more than 75% of the globe. Moreover, since the "third world" occupies a place in the first, we might now be said to have a worldwide point of departure. The multicultural population mix has a growing need for a polyvalent conception of art, a "different" look at history, changing (power)relationships – also in the arts. I therefore regard a collection based on contemporary art developments from non-western traditions as a vital means of making up for the arrears in the Dutch and European (multi)cultural heritage and making the necessary additions. Let us not forget that contemporary art is the cultural heritage of tomorrow. In addition to assembling collections and establishing new institutions, it is of course extremely important for existing museums to pursue a more truly international policy.

Sadly, the art world's objections to the concept of the Almere Museum killed the initiative. The most vehement attack came from the Dutch art journal *Metropolis M*. In a meeting they convened for journalists and artists, I was accused of turning the problem upside-down: the general opinion was that instead of giving non-western art a separate status, collections should acquire a mix of western and non-western art.[2] The problem is of course the lack of expertise in the field of contemporary non-western art in today's museums and art institutions. This was confirmed in the same *Metropolis M* meeting, during which one critic maintained that in order to judge a work of art from another culture, it was not necessary to study into that culture. He claimed to have sufficient "viewing expertise" to contextualize the artist's work. This arrogant attitude is evident in some of the art criticism in the Netherlands.

With the exhibition and the accompanying book *The Short History: Independence and Liberation Movements in Africa, 1845-1994*, the Nigerian curator and director

2. "Wereldkunst in Almere," *Metropolis M*, no. 6 (1999): 12-16.

of *Documenta XI*, Okwui Enwezor, demonstrates the extent to which Eurocentrism is hampering expertise in the field of non-western art.[3] He offers viewers and readers historical texts about the African wars for independence and their consequences for the African continent, and an overview of forms of cultural expression during that same period. These historical events are closely linked with Europe then and now, but we prefer to forget or conceal them or, worse still, know nothing about them. These events are essential for African self-understanding, but also for that of Europeans and Americans, whose lives were so closely interwoven for centuries and still are, due to colonization, slavery and migration. This history accounts for the most important chapters in African history books, but is rarely discussed in European history books. The European twentieth-century historical perspective is quite different from that of Africa, as the title of the exhibition expresses in a nutshell. It comes from the English historian Eric Hobsbawm, who outlines twentieth-century world history in the framework of two monumental European events, the first world war (1914) and the fall of the Berlin Wall (1991).[4] Enwezor has corrected this Eurocentric view of the world by confronting it with an African perspective: for Africa, the most important period of the twentieth century was marked by the wars of independence waged against the west. Accordingly, his "Short Century" is between 1945 and 1994.

The exhibition teaches us that art cannot be seen separately from power-relationships, political developments and economic and social facts. This makes art both fascinating and challenging, since it suggests that the arrears of non-western art in our collections must be dealt with not only by accumulating objects, but also by gaining expertise. The problem cannot be solved by presenting four Chinese artists in the main show at the Venice biennial, nor by publishing reviews by ignorant art critics. Critics ought to think more seriously about art in context and take into account politics, and anthropological and social circumstances. In addition, newspapers and art magazines should invite non-western art critics, from the Diaspora and from the regions concerned, the Sudan, China or Trinidad, to review

3. Okwui Enwezor (ed.), *The Short History: Independence and Liberation Movements in Africa, 1945-1994*, (Munich: Villa Stuck Museum; Munich, London, New York: Prestel Verlag, 2001).
4. Eric Hobsbawm, *Age of Extremes. The Short Twentieth Century, 1914-1991* (London: 1994).

exhibitions and point out historical contexts. In view of the communication techniques at our disposal, this is getting easier all the time. Museum practice in the twenty-first century must become both "inclusive" (a Senegalese curator in the Stedelijk Museum) and "exclusive" (forming a collection based on a historically relevant practice towards non-western art and an educational practice targeting, say, Chinese, Turkish or North African cultural history) to write a truly global history.

Lectures and Debates Witte de With

November 2000 – December 2001

November 30, 2000
Carel Blotkamp, Sebastian Lopez and Bartomeu Marí
The Netherlands Imagined

January 25, 2001
Thomas Levin
Heterochronicity

February 22, 2001
Bart Lootsma, Siebe Thissen and Camiel van Winkel
Art on Location

May 17, 2001
Jeroen Boomgaard and Koen Brams
Good Art doesn't need Theory?

May 31, 2001
Iwona Blazwick and Catherine David
The New Curator

June 22, 2001
Katalin Herzog, Adi Martis and Els van der Plas
Moderator: Ineke Schwartz
The Boundaries of World Art #1

November 27, 2001
Anthony Dunne, Fiona Raby and Alan Murray
Design Noir

December 6, 2001
Charlotte Huygens, Janneke Wesseling and Kitty Zijlmans
The Boundaries of World Art #2

Biographies

Iwona Blazwick

Jeroen Boomgaard

Koen Brams

Valentijn Byvanck

Catherine David

(1955) is director of Whitechapel Art Gallery in London. She was head of exhibitions and display at Tate Modern, London, visiting tutor at the Royal College of Art, London, and director of exhibitions at London's Institute of Contemporary Arts. She was editor of the *Tate Modern Handbook* (London: Tate Gallery Publishing, 2000) and *Century City: Art and Culture in the Modern Metropolis* (London: Tate Gallery Publishing, 2001), and is a critic and broadcaster contributing reviews and commentaries for television and radio.

(1953) teaches contemporary art and theory at the University of Amsterdam, and the Eindhoven University of Technology. He also taught at the Curatorial Training Program of De Appel, Amsterdam. Boomgaard publishes regularly on contemporary art and the art of the 1960s.

(1964) is director of the Jan van Eyck Academy, Maastricht, and former editor of the only Dutch-language journal of art theory, *De Witte Raaf*. He also edited *De Encyclopedie van Fictieve Kunstenaars* [The encyclopedia of fictive artists] (Amsterdam: Nijgh & Van Ditmar, 2000; Boston: David Godine, 2003).

(1964) is in charge of Theory and Communications at Witte de With.

(1954) is director of Witte de With. She was curator at Musée Nationale d'Art Moderne Centre Georges Pompidou, and at Galerie Nationale du Jeu de Paume, both in Paris. In 1994, she was appointed as director of *Documenta X* in Kassel, Germany, which opened in 1997. David worked as a guest curator for numerous international institutions and programs.

Anthony Dunne

Charlotte Huygens

Bart Lootsma

Alan Murray

(1964) is a senior research fellow in Computer Related Design and a senior tutor in Design Products at the Royal College of Art, London. His work has been exhibited at the Centre Georges Pompidou in Paris, the Axis Gallery in Tokyo, and the Design Museum in London. He is author of *Hertzian Tales: Electronic Products, Aesthetic Experience and Critical Design* (London: RCA CRD Research Publications, 1999). In 1992, he formed a partnership with Fiona Raby to explore interrelationships between industrial design, architecture and electronic media through a combination of academic research and practical commissions. With Raby, he authored *Design Noir: The Secret Life of Electronic Objects* (Basel: Birkhäuser, 2002).

(1964) is curator arts and the Islamic world at the World Arts Museum in Rotterdam and author of "Recent werk van twaalf Arabische Kunstenaars" [recent works by twelve Arab artists], in: *Midden-Oosten & Noord-Afrika tijdschrift Soera* [Journal about the Middle East and North Africa, Soera].

(1957) is a historian, critic and curator in the fields of architecture, design and the visual arts. He is a visiting professor for architectural history and theory at the University of Applied Arts in Vienna, and thesis-tutor at the Berlage Institute in Rotterdam. He is an editor of *Archis,* member of the scientific committee of ArchiLab in Orléans, curator of the Schneider Forberg Foundation in Munich and Crown Member of the Dutch Culture Council. He is author of *SuperDutch,* on recent architecture in the Netherlands (London: Thames & Hudson, 2000; Nijmegen: SUN, 2000), and *Body & Globe,* a collection of essays (Rotterdam: 010 Publishers, 2002).

(1965) artist, in charge of the entertainment department in the industrial design faculty at the Eindhoven Institute of Technology. He also teaches at the Rietveld Academy in Amsterdam and is author of www.guide-to-squash.org.

Els van der Plas

Fiona Raby

Janneke Wesseling

Camiel van Winkel

(1960) is art historian, curator and critic. She is director of the Prince Claus Fund which stimulates and supports activities in the field of culture and development. In 1988, she founded the Gate Foundation, an organization for the intercultural exchange of contemporary art. Van der Plas is author and editor of various publications, including *Indonesian Modern Art / Indonesische moderne kunst* (Amsterdam: Gate Foundation, 1993).

(1963) is lecturer and researcher at the Royal College of Art, London. She collaborated with Pierre d'Avoine Architects on Japanese projects such as Air Bar and Tsudanuma City and received an Arts Council research grant for *ICi* an installation for the exchange of cultural information in 1993. In 1992, she formed a partnership with Anthony Dunne to explore interrelationships between industrial design, architecture and electronic media through a combination of academic research and practical commissions. With Dunne, she authored *Design Noir: The Secret Life of Electronic Objects* (Basel: Birkhäuser, 2002).

(1955) has been art critic for *NRC Handelsblad* since 1993, and lecturer art theory at the art academy of The Hague since 1996. In addition to having published a large number of articles about modern and contemporary art, Wesseling published two books: *Alles was mooi. Een geschiedenis van de Nulbeweging* [Everything was Beautiful. A History of the Nul-Movement] (Amsterdam: Meulenhoff/Landshoff, 1989) and *Schoonhoven, beeldend kunstenaar* [Schoonhoven, visual artist] (The Hague/Amsterdam: SDU/Openbaar Kunstbezit, 1990).

(1964) is critic, essayist and editor at *De Witte Raaf* and author of *Moderne leegte. Over kunst en openbaarheid* [Modern Emptiness: About Art and Publicness] (Nijmegen: SUN 1999).

Kitty Zijlmans

(1955) is professor in the history and theory of the modern visual arts, University of Leiden, and chair of the art history department's curriculum committee devoted to creating a world arts program. She is author and editor of various publications, among which: Marlite Halbertsma and Kitty Zijlmans (eds.), *Gezichtspunten. Een inleiding in de methoden van de kunstgeschiedenis* [Perspectives: An Introduction into the Methods of Art History] (Nijmegen: SUN, 1993; Berlin: Reimer Verlag, 1995).

Editor
Valentijn Byvanck

Copy editing and production
Solange de Boer

Design
Gracia Lebbink

Typesetting
Willem Morelis

Translations
Ruth König
Maudi Quandt (Camiel van Winkel)

Transcriptions
Herman Verhagen

Photographs
Bob Goedewaagen
Jean-Pierre Le Blanc (Koen Brams)
Nienke Terpsma
HY (Camiel van Winkel)

Printed by
Die Keure, Bruges, Belgium

Publisher
Witte de With, center for contemporary art,
Rotterdam

ISBN: 90-73362-54-7

Printed and bound in Belgium

Witte de With, center for contemporary art
Witte de Withstraat 50
3012 BR Rotterdam
(t) +31 (0)10 4110144
(f) +31 (0)10 4117924
(e) info@wdw.nl
(i) www.wdw.nl

Staff
Director: Catherine David; Adjunct-director: Paul van Gennip; Curators: Tanja Elstgeest, Nathalie Zonnenberg; Communication and Theory: Valentijn Byvanck; Publications: Solange de Boer; Education: Belinda Hak; Internet: Ariadne Urlus; Assistent to the Director: Carolien Ruigrok; Office: Yvonne van de Griendt, Mariëtte Maaskant and Erik Visser; Reception: Mariëlle Wichards, Marlieke Wijnakker; Technical staff: Gé Beckman, Line Kramer.

Witte de With is an initiative of the Rotterdam Arts Council and is supported by the City of Rotterdam and the Dutch Ministry of Culture.

Distribution
Distribution International: Idea Books,
Nieuwe Herengracht 11, 1011 RK Amsterdam,
The Netherlands
(t) +31 20 6226154; (f) +31 20 6209299;
(e) idea@ideabooks.nl

Distribution in the United Kingdom:
Cornerhouse, 70 Oxford Street, Manchester M1 5NH,
England
(t) +44 161 2001503; (f) +44 161 2001504;
(e) publications@cornerhouse.org

Distribution in North, South and Central America:
D.A.P./Distributed Art Publishers Inc.,
155 Sixth Avenue, 2nd floor, New York, NY 10013-1507, USA
(t) +1 212 627 1999; (f) +1 212 627 9484